IMAGES
of Aviation

TETERBORO AIRPORT

IMAGES
of Aviation

TETERBORO AIRPORT

Henry M. Holden

ARCADIA
PUBLISHING

Published by Arcadia Publishing
Charleston SC, Chicago IL, Portsmouth NH, San Francisco CA

Library of Congress Control Number: 2009930317

For all general information contact Arcadia Publishing at:
Telephone 843-853-2070
Fax 843-853-0044
E-mail sales@arcadiapublishing.com
For customer service and orders:
Toll-Free 1-888-313-2665

Visit us on the Internet at www.arcadiapublishing.com

WITTEMANN AIRCRAFT AND NEW YORK AIR TERMINAL CORPORATION
Teterboro, (Hasbrouck Heights) New Jersey
"NEITHER SNOW NOR RAIN, STORM OR FAIR, SHALL STAY THE COURIERS OF THE AIR"

WITTEMANN AIRCRAFT AND NEW YORK AIR TERMINAL CORPORATION. Looking east, this is an artist's rendition of what Teterboro Airport could grow to be. It included dirigible hangars on the left, two large Wittemann Aircraft Company buildings in the lower right, and plans to carve a roadway to the Hackensack River to test amphibian airplanes the Wittemanns had planned to build. (New Jersey Aviation Hall of Fame and Museum.)

CONTENTS

ACKNOWLEDGMENTS

A book is never the product of one person but a collaborative effort of many. In this case, I am appreciative to Shea Oakley, executive director of the New Jersey Aviation Hall of Fame and Museum (NJAHOF) for allowing me access to the archives where I found most of the photographs for this book. I am also grateful to H. V. "Pat" Reilly, director emeritus and cofounder of the NJAHOF, for his review of this manuscript and the use of his book *From the Balloon to the Moon* as a major reference, along with many unpublished archival records. Rudy Steinthal and Steve Riethof were helpful in their review of the manuscript for technical accuracy. Without these gentlemen, this book would not have been possible. Any errors are the result of my fiddling with the manuscript after their review.

I also want to acknowledge my wife and best friend, Nancy, for putting up with my passion for writing.

INTRODUCTION

Teterboro Airport, located in Bergen County, New Jersey, is situated just south of Hackensack at the edge of the Hackensack Meadowlands, 12 miles from Midtown Manhattan.

Teterboro Airport, called the "cradle of the golden age of aviation," has been in continuous use since 1916, and at one point, it was considered the busiest airport in the country with 1,000 daily movements. Located just 18 miles north of Newark Liberty International Airport, Teterboro served a different role from its neighbor in the development of aviation. Teterboro's heritage includes the hundreds of general-aviation developments and records established there and the men and women who created them.

Around 1825, the land was described as "more than half salt marsh and cedar swamps." Dutch farmers drained off portions of the land by digging ditches and developed a modest crop-producing soil.

In 1917, Walter C. Teter acquired the swampy property. Today the town of Teterboro is the smallest municipality in Bergen County and has a synergistic relationship with the airport, which is the largest tract of land in the borough.

The first attempts at aviation at Teterboro barely got off the ground. In 1910, Frederick Kuhnert and a friend bought a 20-acre plot of land to use as an airfield. Kuhnert built an airplane that could hold 14 passengers. Called *Kuhnert's Ferryboat*, it was destroyed in 1912 in a tornado before it flew. Prior to the tornado, the Kuhnert Aerodrome hosted weekly air demonstrations.

Charles, Paul, Adolph, and Walter Wittemann, who founded the first airplane manufacturing plant in the United States on Staten Island in 1905, bought the meadowland from Teter. In 1918, they built a manufacturing plant and opened the Wittemann-Lewis Aircraft Company with Samuel P. Lewis. They acquired a post office contract to convert surplus U.S. Army deHavilland DH-4 aircraft for the first airmail service. Approximately 75 to 100 aircraft were modified at the plant.

After Lewis left the company, in 1920, the Wittemann Aircraft Company won a fixed-price contract to build the army's Barling Bomber, a three winged, 10 wheeled, six-engine bomber that at the time was the largest airplane in the world. The army made many design changes but ultimately rejected the bomber. With a combined 15,600 horsepower, its top speed was only 90 miles per hour empty. The army refused to pay the Wittemanns the $250,000 balance on the contract, and that forced them out of business. They subsequently leased their plant to Anthony Fokker, the world-famous Dutch aircraft designer. Fokker made his reputation during World War I as the builder of aircraft for the German Air Force, among them Manfred "Red Baron" von Richthofen's triplane.

In 1925, Fokker opened the Atlantic Aircraft Corporation in the Wittemann hangar. For the next few years, Teterboro-built Fokker trimotors dominated the aviation industry, but they were sent to the dustbin in March 1931, when famed football coach Knute Rockne died in a Fokker F-10 when it lost a wing.

In the 1920s and 1930s, record-setting flights became a national obsession, and many of the flights originated or terminated at Teterboro Airport. In 1926, navy commander Richard E. Byrd and warrant officer Floyd Bennett flew a Fokker F-VII trimotor over the North Pole and back in 15½ hours for a total of 1,334 nautical miles.

In 1926, Juan Terry Trippe, a Yale College graduate, saw the future of commercial aviation. He formed Colonial Air Transport (CAT), based at Hadley Field in South Plainfield and Teterboro. CAT received the first airmail contract awarded to private aviation, Route No. 1 between Boston and New York (Teterboro). Trippe chose two Fokker F-VIIs and a single-engine Curtiss Lark for his new airmail service. On July 1, CAT inaugurated scheduled service, with the three airplanes leaving Hadley Field at 6:10 a.m. They touched down in Boston at 9:35 a.m. On the return trip that evening, the pilots landed at Teterboro and found Tripp and a crowd of 20,000 waiting to cheer them. CAT went into the passenger business in 1927, and on October 28, 1927, Trippe founded Pan American World Airways (Pan Am), with a Teterboro-built Fokker F-VII trimotor on his international route from Key West, Florida, to Havana, Cuba.

The major aviation challenge in the 1920s was to fly the Atlantic Ocean nonstop. Raymond Orteig, a wealthy businessperson, offered a prize of $25,000 to the first person who completed a nonstop flight between New York and Paris. A number of aviators had tried both east and west bound, but all had failed.

In 1927, there were three strong contenders for the prize: Byrd, Clarence D. Chamberlin, and Charles A. Lindbergh. Byrd had experience flying a Fokker trimotor over the North Pole and planned to fly another Fokker trimotor, the *America*, to cross the Atlantic.

In April 1927, during a test flight of *America* at Teterboro Airport, the airplane crashed on landing. Fokker was at the controls, and Floyd Bennett, Byrd, and a radioman were passengers. All survived the crash, although Bennett was severely injured. The *America* was repaired, but the accident was a setback for Byrd. *America* became the third aircraft to fly nonstop to Europe, almost a month after Lindbergh's flight.

On May 20, 1927, Lindbergh flew from Roosevelt Field in New York and became the first person to cross the Atlantic nonstop. He was an instant worldwide hero and became the face of American aviation.

Chamberlin logged over 35,800 hours of flight time during his 27 years in the air, mostly as a captain with Pan Am. He first learned to fly at Teterboro. Chamberlin teamed up with Giuseppe Bellanca, an aircraft designer who worked for the Wright brothers, and millionaire Charles A. Levine. Levine bought a Bellanca monoplane and decided to go for the Orteig prize.

In early April 1927, to test the endurance of the Bellanca monoplane, Chamberlin and his copilot Bert Acosta set an endurance record of 51 hours 11 minutes and beat the old record by nearly six hours. Bellanca was thrilled and believed his airplane *Miss Columbia* could successfully cross the Atlantic. However, Levine changed his mind and got Acosta to quit and join Byrd's party. Two weeks after Lindbergh's flight, Chamberlin, with Levine as the first transatlantic passenger, flew the Bellanca from New York to Cottbus, Germany. Their trip was the longest nonstop flight then recorded.

When Chamberlin returned to the United States, the United States Steamship Line asked him to attempt to fly the mail off a special 80-foot runway constructed on the S.S. *Leviathan*. Chamberlin took off successfully and flew the first ship-to-shore mail to Teterboro Airport.

Along with the rest of the country, the Great Depression dealt Teterboro a serious economic blow. Aviation activities dried up. The Fokker factory became a dance hall and fight arena, and efforts were made to turn the fledgling airport into a sports center and racetrack.

It was during this period that Bergen County police chief Peter Siccardi and Clyde Pangborn formed the first flying police unit in the United States. Siccardi had won national acclaim when he directed vehicular traffic by semaphore signals from aloft during an air show at Teterboro. He used the same Fokker airplane Chamberlin had flown from the S.S. *Leviathan*.

In 1937, Vincent Bendix bought 100 acres of land adjacent to the field and built the Eclipse-Pioneer Division of the Bendix Aviation Corporation. Soon the Bendix plant was attracting new business to the airport's sod runway. For a few years, it was called Bendix Airport. In 1943, voters changed the name back to Teterboro Airport.

In 1939, Teterboro became a blimp base. The Goodyear blimp *Mayflower* made daily sightseeing and advertising flights over the New York World's Fair and northern New Jersey.

In 1941, a former Marine Corps pilot Fred L. Wehran bought Teterboro. He had plans for developing an air cargo center, but World War II put his plans on hold when the U.S. Army Airforce closed the field to civilian traffic.

In 1946, the army released the airport back to Wehran, who continued to make improvements. He installed the first control tower, a gondola perched atop a wood-framed building. He later convinced the Federal Aviation Administration (FAA) to build a modern tower on the north end of the Atlantic Aviation Corporation hangar. It became the first home of the Aviation Hall of Fame and Museum at Teterboro in 1972.

As airfreight traffic continued to grow, Wehran paved two 3,000-foot runways. Teterboro was becoming the world's busiest airfreight terminal. To alleviate the yearly springtime flooding, water pumps were installed in the marshlands.

With the improvements made, large corporations began to move in and industrial parks began to rise in the surrounding areas. Teterboro was slowly becoming a force to be reckoned with and a major player in air commerce.

In 1946, the Atlantic Aviation Corporation became the largest fixed-base operator (FBO) on the field when it moved a branch of its Wilmington, Delaware, organization into Teterboro. In 1981, Atlantic Aviation Corporation opened a new modern hangar and terminal/office complex on the west side of the airfield and doubled its capacity to service aircraft.

During the postwar period, Teterboro, because of its close proximity to New York City, became a viable alternative to the crowded Newark and LaGuardia Airports. Teterboro became an ideal location to base corporate aircraft to relieve traffic at Newark and LaGuardia.

Realizing the importance of Teterboro to the region, the Port Authority of New York opened negotiations with Wehran to buy the property. In 1949, the port authority purchased the airport for $3 million. It invested $10.5 million to further lengthen the runways and equipped one of them with an instrument landing system (ILS). For a period, the port authority operated the airport through contractors but today manages it directly.

In 1949, World War II flying ace William Odom became one of the many people who helped create the Teterboro Airport legacy by flying a Beechcraft Bonanza 4,285 miles nonstop from Honolulu, Hawaii, to Teterboro. Immediately after his spectacular flight, Odom opened an executive air service and a restaurant on the west side of the airfield, but he was killed later that year in an air race.

Dozens of notable people used Teterboro over the years, but one of them brought national attention to the airport: television personality Arthur Godfrey, who based his private aircraft at Teterboro. In 1952, the FAA accused Godfrey of purposely buzzing the control tower while taking off in his DC-3. The incident took place during his prime as a radio and television variety show host. Godfrey carried on a televised verbal battle with the FAA, which lasted more than a year and attracted millions of viewers. Later found guilty, he had his pilot's license revoked for six months. In 1966, Godfrey went on to set a round-the-world record of 86 hours in a jet commander based at Teterboro.

In 1965, the port authority and Pan Am signed an agreement to authorize the airline to manage Teterboro for the agency under the direction of Capt. O. J. Studeman, a veteran Pan Am pilot and executive. When Studeman was asked why Pan Am wanted to operate Teterboro, he replied, "to develop Teterboro as a first-class general aviation airport to help alleviate growing air-traffic congestion at Metropolitan New York's three commercial jetports, and to assist in meeting the needs of general aviation pilots and passengers."

Pan Am invested $10 million to lengthen, widen, and overlay the runways. It constructed taxiways and built a large hangar complex at the south end of the field. It added visual approach aids, and these improvements brought more business to the airport.

By the 1970s, Teterboro was more prosperous than at any time in its history. In 1971, the year after Pan Am assumed management, 9,775 movements were recorded at the airport. By 1975, it was up to 18,375.

Because Teterboro Airport is located in a highly populated area and shares airspace with LaGuardia, John F. Kennedy International, and Newark Airports, a dynamic air show is difficult to arrange and coordinate safely. The last dynamic air show at Teterboro, a two-day event held in 1973, attracted over 25,000 people. Today there is an annual Wings and Wheels Expo, a static show, each fall.

In 1975, the FAA moved from the control tower attached to the Atlantic Aviation hangar to a new, modern facility on the east side of the airport. It was then that the Aviation Hall of Fame and Museum at Teterboro and Pan Am signed a contract permitting the use of the top three floors of the tower as a hall of fame and museum. Today the hall of fame has its own building on the east side of the field adjacent to the control tower.

One

THE EARLY YEARS
1917–1944

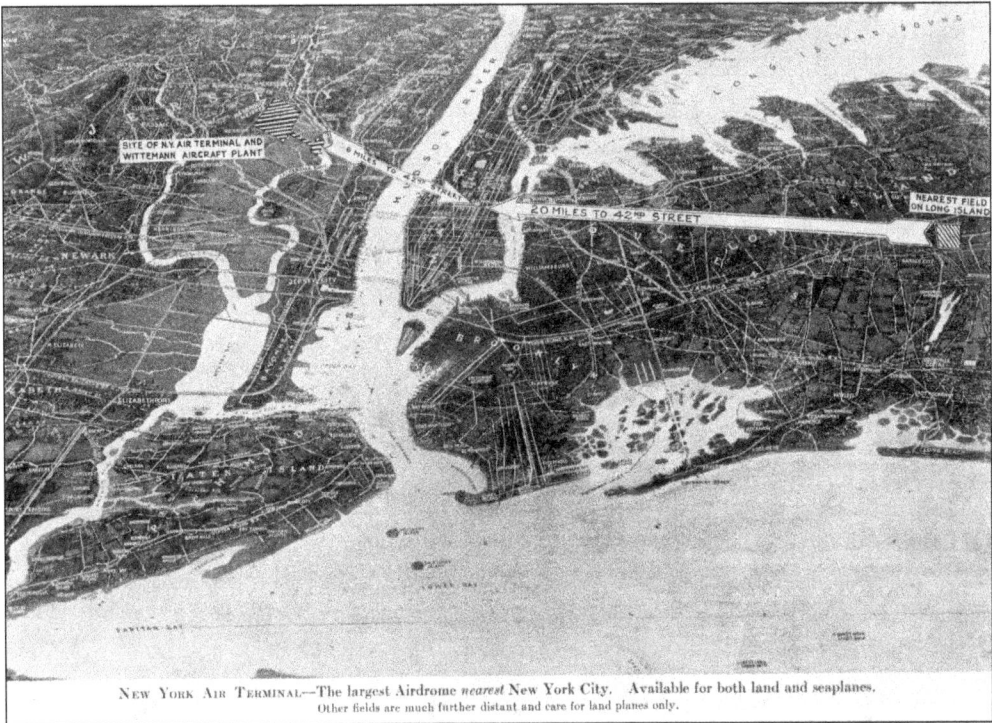

NEW YORK AIR TERMINAL.—The largest Airdrome *nearest* New York City. Available for both land and seaplanes. Other fields are much further distant and care for land planes only.

CLOSE TO NEW YORK CITY. This artist's drawing promoted the proximity of the Wittemann-Lewis Aircraft Company and the New York Air Terminal to New York City. The name New York Air Terminal was short-lived. The idea, while it looked good on paper, could not sustain any serious aviation settlement while the land remained undrained. (NJAHOF.)

FREDRICK KUHNERT. In 1910, Frederick Kuhnert bought 20 acres of land in the Hackensack Meadowlands to use as an aerodrome. Kuhnert built a passenger airplane that could hold 14 people. Called *Kuhnert's Ferryboat*, it, along with his aerodrome, was destroyed by a tornado in 1912 before it could take its first flight. (NJAHOF.)

TWO WITTEMANN BROTHERS. Two of the Wittemann brothers, Charles (left) and Adolph are seated in a 1908 Wittemann design. Although aviation came to Teterboro with the Wittemanns, pilots did not use the grass airstrip until William Diehl landed his English Avro there on August 13, 1920. (NJAHOF.)

WITTEMANN AIRCRAFT COMPANY FACTORY. This is the Wittemann Aircraft Company factory around 1919. Note the absence of any aircraft. This photograph shows the field before Wittemann got a government contract to convert deHavilland DH-4s for airmail service. The dirt road in front of the plant eventually became Industrial Avenue. Malcolm Avenue was carved behind the plant. The undeveloped land to the left became Teterboro Airport. (NJAHOF.)

WITTEMANN XNBL-1 BARLING BOMBER. In 1920, the Wittemann Aircraft Company won an army contract to build the Barling Bomber, a three winged, six-engine (two inboard engines had pusher engines in tandem) bomber that was at the time the largest airplane in the world. The undercarriage consisted of 10 wheels, including two wheels mounted on the front of the aircraft (to prevent a nose-over on landing). Its first flight was on August 22, 1923. (NJAHOF.)

13

WITTEMANN FACTORY. This is the Wittemann Aircraft Company factory as it looked around 1920. The numerous design changes demanded by the army and a fixed-price contract for the Barling Bomber forced Wittemann out of business. The company leased the plant to Anthony Fokker in 1924. Note the pooled water that was an issue after every heavy rain for decades. (NJAHOF.)

FLOODED TETERBORO. Water obliterates the meadowlands in this undated photograph. This condition is a major reason why Teterboro Airport never competed successfully with its neighbor Newark Airport, 18 miles to the south, in the early days of their existences. It was not until pumps were installed that Teterboro Airport became viable. (NJAHOF.)

RUTH LAW. On August 1, 1912, Ruth Law (right) soloed. She received her license on November 12, 1912, and immediately went to work as a commercial pilot, flying passengers in Florida. Seen here with passenger Mrs. Robert Goelet of New York City, Law was one of the early pilots who flew exhibition flights at the short-lived Kuhnert Aerodrome. (Author's collection.)

ITINERANT PILOT. William Diehl was a movie stunt pilot and flight instructor. In 1919, he established the first flying taxi service. In 1930, Diehl flew parachutist Berne LaBalta up 17,500 feet in a Curtiss Robin monoplane. LaBalta jumped over Teterboro, setting the altitude jump record for that time. (NJAHOF.)

WITTEMANN BROTHERS. In 1905, Charles, Paul, Adolph, and Walter Wittemann founded the first airplane manufacturing plant in the United States on Staten Island. In 1917, they bought some of the meadowland from Walter C. Teter and established the first aircraft factory at Teterboro in 1918. Three of the brothers, Paul, Charles, and Walter, were elected to the Aviation Hall of Fame and Museum at Teterboro in 1972. (Author's collection.)

WITTEMANN AIRCRAFT MAIL SERVICE. In 1919, the Wittemann brothers received a post office contract to convert U.S. Army Air Service DH-4 airplanes to be able to carry 400 to 1,000 pounds of mail. The Wittemann brothers modified about 100 airplanes. This photograph shows the Hasbrouck Heights railroad station in the background. The station is gone, but the rail line is still active. (NJAHOF.)

TIDAL WETLANDS. This 1920s photograph, taken from the Wittemann factory roof, shows three airplanes on the right in water. In 1916, the lowland on the edge of the Hackensack Meadowlands attracted the French government, seeking suitable training fields for Allied pilots. Teterboro failed to make the cut after officials noted that each heavy rainstorm turned the site into a sea of mud. (NJAHOF.)

MINUTES FROM MANHATTAN. One of the earliest photographs of Teterboro shows a pastoral landscape. Teterboro began as 670 acres of swampland purchased shortly after the dawn of the 20th century by Riser Land Company. Walter C. Teter, who owned Riser, wanted to build a racetrack. Under a special state law enacted in 1917, the borough was established to accommodate the racetrack. Before the state completed its review of Teter's plan, Teter sold a large portion of the property to Whiteman-Lewis Aircraft Company. (NJAHOF.)

PASTORAL TETERBORO. In 1920, the Wittemann Aircraft Company plant was one of the largest in the United States. It converted World War I biplanes to carry airmail. When Anthony Fokker took over in 1924, the pastoral setting changed into a growing and thriving airport. Fokker became one of the largest airplane manufacturers in the United States until 1930. (NJAHOF.)

STANDARD J-1. The Curtiss JN-4 Jenny and the Standard J-1 biplane, pictured here, were stable mates and competitors for the mail contracts and were the choice of air show performers. They were made of fabric, wood, and wire bracings (needed for the wings), which led some to nickname them "string bags." This is a J-1 rebuilt as a Lincoln Standard in 1921 with a Hispano engine. It cost about $13,000. (NJAHOF.)

NEW STANDARD AIRCRAFT DESTROYED. On June 7, 1931, pilot George J. De Garmo Jr., manager of the New Standard Flying Service at Teterboro, crashed after takeoff, injuring him and three passengers. Several thousand people who were watching stunt flying and parachute jumping witnessed the accident. The New Jersey Aviation Board determined the aircraft was too dangerous and condemned the type. All surviving aircraft were destroyed. (NJAHOF.)

WITTEMANN FACTORY, C. 1921. When Fokker took over the Wittemann factory in 1924, he ramped up production. He employed about 400 men and produced about 200 airplanes a year. The average rate of pay for the men was about to $2.50 per day. In May 1929, General Motors acquired a 40 percent interest in Fokker's company and renamed it the General Aviation Manufacturing Corporation, and Fokker became a technical director. (NJAHOF.)

JOHN (JACK) WEBSTER. In the spring of 1921, the post office asked Charles Wittemann to fly one of his DH-M2 (a modified DH-4) to Washington, D.C., for its consideration for use as a mail airplane. Wittemann and John (Jack) Webster flew from Teterboro to Bowling Field, outside of Washington, D.C., in two hours and 45 minutes. The post office approved the modified airframe. The return trip to Teterboro took two hours and eight minutes. (NJAHOF.)

DEHAVILLAND DH-4. Weeks later, the post office asked Webster to fly to San Francisco with 1,000 pounds of mail. The modified DH-M2 flight took seven days. By the end of the decade, the wear and tear and the high accident rate among airmail pilots and air show performers had decimated the ranks of the DH-4. Pilots and designers were looking for new and safer airframes. (NJAHOF.)

JN-4. The JN-4 Jenny was a World War I training airplane that was pressed into service after the war to jump-start the airmail business. Although these airplanes were frequent visitors to Teterboro for repairs and modifications, the airport could not compete at the same economic level with Newark Airport since it did not have mail contracts with the airlines. (NJAHOF.)

AERIAL REFUELING. Wesley May is carrying a five-gallon gasoline can strapped to his back and is transferring from a New Standard flown by Frank Hawks to a Jenny flown by Earl Daugherty. This was only one of two refueling methods available in the early days of endurance-setting records. The other was a hose from one airplane to the other, a method that is still in use, although now more sophisticated. (NJAHOF.)

21

HELLER FIELD. Heller Field was located in the North Ward of Newark and began operations in December 1919 as an airmail field. Landing at Heller Field was dangerous because a canal, a tall factory chimney, and a railroad surrounded it. There were so many accidents and 26 fatalities that the post office closed the field in May 1921, taking it out of competition with Teterboro. (NJAHOF.)

ADJUSTING A PARACHUTE BALLOON. In this 1922 photograph, Wesley May is seen adjusting the harness on an exhibition parachute balloon with pilot Lowell Yerex. Both men were performers with the Gates Flying Circus. Notice Yerex is dressed completely in leather to insulate himself against the cold wind in an open-cockpit biplane. (NJAHOF.)

SWAMPLANDS TO AIRPORT, C. 1928. Teterboro Airport, which grew from swampland in the boroughs of Moonachie and Teterboro in Bergen County, has been in constant use since about 1916. North American Aviation used it during World War I as an aircraft-manufacturing site and afterwards as a base of operations for aircraft designers Charles Wittemann and Anthony Fokker. (NJAHOF.)

WRIGHT AERONAUTICAL HANGAR. Teterboro Airport is the oldest operating airport in the New York and New Jersey metropolitan area and today is the sixth busiest general-aviation airport in the nation. It has remained in the top 10 busiest airports since the 1950s. (NJAHOF.)

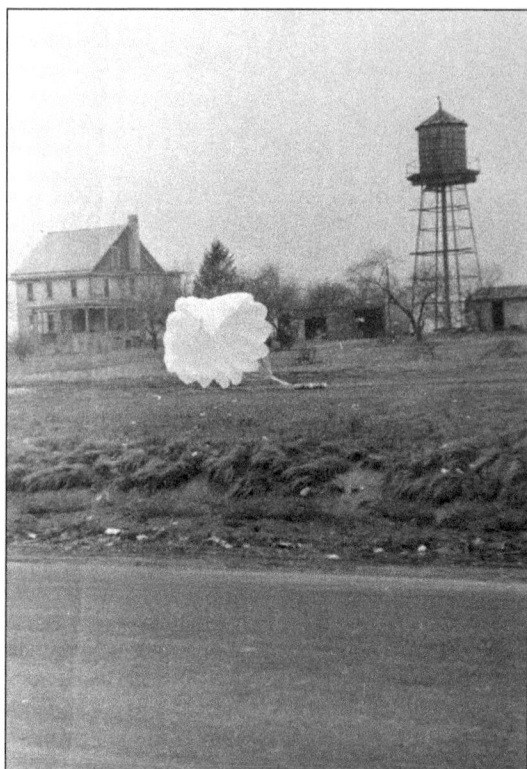

PARACHUTE FLARE. At night and before airport lighting in rain, fog, or an emergency, airmail pilots dropped a parachute flare to see if they were over the airport and tried to land by its light. This flare came down just outside the airport, and it is unknown if it helped or hindered the pilot's landing. Two flares were usually carried. (NJAHOF.)

FOKKER F-32 WING. Nearly a dozen workers are busy building the massive wing of the Fokker F-32. Anthony Fokker called his plant the Atlantic Aircraft Corporation and assembled Dutch-made parts until he built up a production line with designs made by his American team. The F-10 was the first model produced in the United States. His trimotors and other types dominated the U.S. aviation market for years. (NJAHOF.)

FLOYD BENNETT. Floyd Bennett came to Teterboro in the mid-1920s to test fly the Fokker trimotor aircraft used by Adm. Richard E. Byrd on his Arctic and Atlantic flights. Badly injured in a test flight accident at Teterboro, Bennett subsequently caught pneumonia on a mercy flight to rescue the aircraft *Bremen* on Greeneley Island, Newfoundland, and died. (NJAHOF.)

CAR-TO-AIRPLANE CHANGE. Clyde Pangborn is about to transfer from a car speeding along at 65 miles per hour to a rope ladder trailing behind a JN-4 Jenny. Moments later, Pangborn lost his grip on the ladder and fell to the ground. He was seriously injured, but the accident did not dissuade him from staying in the game. When the air shows took place at Teterboro, an ambulance from nearby Hasbrouck Heights Hospital was always standing by. (NJAHOF.)

FOKKER PLANT. When the former Wittemann-Lewis Aircraft Company plant opened in 1917, it had a 120-foot-by-200-foot long, 30-foot-high assembly floor. At the time, it was the largest aircraft factory in the country. Shortly after it opened, Samuel P. Lewis resigned from the company, and it became the Wittemann Aircraft Company. When Fokker took over the building, he stenciled his name on the building both for the attention of incoming pilots and as an advertising tool. (NJAHOF.)

FOKKER F-VII TRIMOTOR. The Fokker F-VII was the most prolific record setter of the 1920s. Fokker put his name on the fuselage and wings of every airplane to distinguish himself from Henry Ford's Tri-Motor. When Comdr. Richard E. Byrd and Floyd Bennett flew the F-VII to the North Pole in 1926, they became world famous overnight. Fokker's aircraft helped establish Teterboro Airport and New Jersey as the East Coast nucleus of aviation development. (NJAHOF.)

WING WALKING SAFELY. Gates Flying Circus wing walker, pilot, and all-around daredevil Aron "Duke" Krantz (right) and a friend demonstrate wing walking the safe way, on the ground, sans wind and the long fall. The Wright hangar is to the left. Note the habitually flooded field in those days. (NJAHOF.)

DOOMED FLIGHT. A Fokker Universal *Old Glory* is being prepared at Teterboro Airport in 1927 for a trip from which it did not return. The airplane was lost at sea on an ill-fated flight from New York to Rome. Pilots James Hill, Lloyd Bertaud, and sponsor Philip Payne, the managing editor of the *New York Daily Mirror*, went down with the airplane. (NJAHOF.)

From the Trans-Continental

GATES FLYING CIRCUS

of San Francisco, California.

("The Daddy of Them All")

We will be glad to get acquainted with eastern flying folks at the Pulitzer Races

Gates Flying Circus

New Eastern Office Address:-

Room, 735, 17 Battery Place, New York City

GATES FLYING CIRCUS. The Gates Flying Circus was called "the Granddaddy of them All." It arrived at Teterboro in 1926 after a five year coast-to-coast tour. During this time, it covered 41 states and visited 1,042 cities. It performed 1,836 exhibitions and flew 100,228 people. At the top of the flyer, on the left is Clyde Pangborn; Ivan Gates is on the right. (NJAHOF.)

GATES FLYER. When the Gates Flying Circus came to Teterboro, it had mostly modified Standard JR-1 biplanes designed by Charles Healy Day. They were painted bright red with a Texaco logo on each side of the fuselage and on each low wing. Texaco supplied the fuel and oil free to all the Gates airplanes. The Standard JR-1 is considered the first commercial aircraft in the United States flown on a regular basis. (NJAHOF.)

28

HADLEY FIELD. Hadley Field was about 26 miles southwest of Teterboro. Newark Airport, Teterboro Airport, and Hadley Field all initially competed for the lucrative airmail contracts. Airmail service never caught on at Teterboro because of drainage problems or at Hadley because it was too far from New York City. National Air Transport has Douglas M-1 mail planes parked in front of its hangar. (NJAHOF.)

SOGGY AIR SHOW. Hundreds of cars line the roadways, and a crowd gathers on a dry spot of land for an air show in 1925. The former Wittemann building and water tower are on the left. By this time, the building was the home of Anthony Fokker and his world-renown airplane company. Fokker enjoyed several years of fame and fortune before the fatal crash of one of his trimotors destroyed his reputation. (NJAHOF.)

GATES FLYING CIRCUS SOUVENIR. When Ivan Gates first made up these souvenirs, they featured the names of the pilots performing at the show. He soon realized that the mortality rate among the wing walkers and airplane changers was so high that he found he could not sell souvenirs of a dead pilot. He then created the generic name "Diavalo" (devil) under which all stunt men and women worked. Aron "Duke" Krantz, featured on this flyer, outlived Gates and the others and passed away 40 years later. (NJAHOF.)

Souvenir of "DIAVALO" (A.F. Krantz) Worlds Master Daredevil with Gates Flying Circus

LOADING AIR MAIL. Hadley Field was the site of the nation's first airmail service and briefly competed with Teterboro Airport until Newark Airport pushed them both aside. Note the pistol on the belt of the person unloading a sack of mail from the forward cockpit. Stealing or interfering with the mail is a federal offense, and the pistol was to discourage such thinking. (NJAHOF.)

BOEING MODEL 40. The first Model 40 was built in 1925 for a U.S. Postal Service competition as a replacement for the converted de Havilland and JN-4 Jenny that had carried the airmail since 1918. The Model 40, which first flew on October 5, 1928, was the major production model of the mail airplane series. It carried up to four passengers and 500 pounds of mail. (NJAHOF.)

COAST-TO-COAST AIR MAIL. This was the start of scheduled night coast-to-coast mail from Hadley Field on July 1, 1925. Fellow airmail pilot James D. Hill (left) congratulates pilot Dean Smith just before Smith took off from the New York terminal (Hadley Field) to Cleveland. Hill took off with a second load later that evening. Engine trouble forced Smith down, but Hill made it to Cleveland. (NJAHOF.)

BERT ACOSTA. Bert Acosta and Clarence D. Chamberlin set the world endurance record for aircraft, staying aloft for 51 hours, 11 minutes in the $25,000 Bellanca WB-2 monoplane *Columbia*. They covered more than 4,100 miles, which was more than the 3,600-mile proposed flight of Chamberlin from New York to Paris. The flight gave Chamberlin the assurance he needed that the aircraft could successfully cross the Atlantic. (NJAHOF.)

ANKLE-DEEP AIR SHOW. This early-1920s photograph show crowds in front of the Wright Aeronautical Corporation hangar for an air show that is virtually underwater. The crowds and vehicles clustered on the only dry ground. Teterboro Airport was at least partially underwater six months out of the year for decades. The airport was on marshlands and subject to the whims of the tides. One company jokingly called themselves the "Ankle Deep Aircraft Company." (NJAHOF.)

CROWDS STORM TETERBORO. Barnstorming was a popular form of entertainment in the 1920s in which stunt pilots performed tricks with airplanes, often in groups called flying circuses. Thousands of people gathered to watch thrilling aerobatics in this 1920s photograph. In the background is the Wittemann factory. From the bunting and flags, this looks like it was probably an Independence Day weekend. (NJAHOF.)

AIRMAIL PILOT CHARLES A. LINDBERGH. Charles A. Lindbergh was an airmail pilot who gained instant fame by becoming the first man to solo across the Atlantic in 1927. He used his fame to become an ardent promoter of commercial aviation. He taught his wife, Anne Morrow Lindbergh, to fly at Teterboro and launched some of his exploration flights from the airport. (Library of Congress.)

GATES LINEUP. The Gates Flying Circus, at the peak of its fame, showed 10 airplanes lined up for the 1927 New York National Airplane Show and Air Circus, held at Teterboro Airport. Accidents and fatalities among air show performers and airmail pilots eventually led to restrictive rules and effectively ended air shows as they were known by the early 1930s. (NJAHOF.)

THUNDERSTORMS. On the evening of September 1, 1927, a thunderstorm rolled through Teterboro and washed out the air show for the following day. The show resumed on September 3. The rains flooded the field, making it necessary to start the events about a quarter mile from the main grandstand. The *New York Times* reported the turnout to be so large that it took two hours for the last motorist to clear the field. (NJAHOF.)

TETERBORO FLOODED AGAIN. This September 2, 1927, photograph looking northeast shows Teterboro Airport flooded from a recent storm. The lack of paved runways on property that was almost at sea level kept the airport virtually undeveloped for decades. The three airplanes on the ground belong to the Gates Flying Circus. (NJAHOF.)

CHAMBERLIN IN GERMANY. Clarence D. Chamberlin (second from left) and Charles A. Levine (right), his passenger on the transatlantic flight, called on German president Paul Von Hindenburg. Jacob Gould, American ambassador to Germany, is in the center. Chamberlin received an enthusiastic reception everywhere he went in Europe. (NJAHOF.)

TOP-BILLED AIR SHOW PERFORMERS. In 1926, Clyde Pangborn (left) and Aron "Duke" Krantz pose alongside a Lincoln Standard belonging to the Gates Flying Circus. The Gates Flying Circus, and other air shows at the time, chased the warmer air south and west during the winter months. Air circuses brought individual barnstormers together for choreographed shows that were marketed well, a technique that has lasted more than 80 years. (NJAHOF.)

IVAN AND HAZEL GATES. The Gates Flying Circus arrived at Teterboro Airport in the summer 1926, after barnstorming almost every state in the Union. Ivan Gates promoted two National Air Show and Air Circus events at Teterboro. His airplanes carried over 750,000 passengers. Gates, seen here with his wife, Hazel, also a pilot, promoted air shows even before World War I. (NJAHOF.)

GATES FLYING CIRCUS AND AVIATION COMPANY

are pleased to announce the opening of their

SCHOOL *of* AVIATION (Division)
at Fokker's Teterboro Airport

Hasbrouck Heights, New Jersey

New York's nearest airdrome seven miles airline—"45 minutes from Broadway" by auto

Bus leaves Hermitage Hotel, 7th Ave. and 42nd St., New York, every hour direct to Field

Greatest Opportunity and Environment Ever Offered a Student

Fokker Aircraft Corporation, Atlantic Aircraft Corporation, Wright Aeronautical Corporation Hangars, United States Air Mail, of Colonial Airways Inc., Clarence D. Chamberlin's home situated on Airport, | Colonel Lindbergh's famous plane now there on exhibition—our own factory and shops immediately adjacent.

See the Giant Fokker Planes Built—See the Famous Wright Whirlwind Motors Tested

Instruction From the Master Pilots of Gates Flying Circus
BY THE LESSON, HOUR OR COMPLETE COURSE—LOW TUITION FEES.

Free ground schooling available to students; actual repairing, rebuilding, rigging, motor work in our own shops, meteorology, navi- | gation, Department of Commerce Laws, Business Tactics of Commercial Aviation.

AMERICA SERIOUSLY NEEDS AVIATORS—LEARN TO FLY *NOW*.

GATES FLYING CIRCUS AND AVIATION CO.
(SCHOOL AND REPAIR DIVISION)

GATES FLYING CIRCUS SCHOOL OF AVIATION. A full-page magazine advertisement announced that Gates was opening a school of aviation at Teterboro Airport. The aim was to lure people from New York City to Teterboro, only 12 miles from Broadway. Whenever the Gates Flying Circus appeared, it drew thousands of young people to the show. The leather jackets, riding britches, and boots worn by the pilots made them iconic stars when they signed programs and photographs for their fans. (NJAHOF.)

WING WALKERS. Ivan Gates, standing on the left, was the general manager of the Gates Flying Circus. A note on the photograph indicates the man on the extreme right died on March 3, presumably soon after the photograph was made. The women are wing walkers who were obviously trained gymnasts as well. (NJAHOF.)

NIGHT TEST FLIGHT. On January 31, 1927, Teterboro Airport launched an airplane carrying mail and two passengers on a 90-minute night test flight, 2,000 feet over Broadway in New York City. The publicity flight was to demonstrate the reliability of the airplane and the efficiency of the instruments used in night airmail flying. (NJAHOF.)

COLONIAL AIR TRANSPORT. This is a Colonial Air Transport (CAT) Keystone Patrician K-78, NX7962. The Keystone K-78 was the largest and fastest trimotor airliner in the United States. CAT flew this 18-passenger prototype on a charter operation from New York to Boston. Only costly and extensive modifications made the aircraft viable for regular service, thus limiting manufacture of this prototype. (NJAHOF.)

38

"UPSIDE DOWN" PANGBORN. Clyde Pangborn hangs by his teeth without a parachute from a New Standard biplane. As parachutist, pilot, and author William (Bill) Rhode said for the title of his book, *Chewing Gum, Bailing Wire and Guts* were used to fly and perform in these dangerous machines. (NJAHOF.)

FOKKER TRIMOTOR. The Fokker trimotors constructed at Teterboro were a mix of materials: metal tubing, doped fabric for the fuselage, and wooden bracing for the wings. Several became famous. Adm. Richard E. Byrd's airplane on his Arctic flight was named *Josephine Ford*. Later he flew *America* as the third man to fly solo across the Atlantic. Another, the *Southern Cross*, flew practically around the world. Juan Trippe used this one on his Havana, Cuba, run. (Author's collection.)

JOSEPHINE FORD. Adm. Richard E. Byrd made one of the most publicized flights (prior to Charles A. Lindbergh's) on May 10, 1926, when he flew near the North Pole in this Fokker trimotor. Instead of putting Fokker's name on the fuselage, which was the practice at the time, Byrd named it the *Josephine Ford* after sponsor Edsel Ford's young daughter. Anthony Fokker still put his name on the airplane wings to garner publicity. (NJAHOF.)

AMERICA. On June 29, 1927, the Teterboro-built Fokker trimotor *America* took off from Roosevelt Field in New York with pilot Brent Balchen and Bert Acosta on board headed for France. The flight carried the first U.S. airmail over the Atlantic Ocean. The weather conditions were so poor that fog over Paris made landing at Le Bourget Airport impossible. The pilots ditched in the Atlantic. The crew and mail survived, but the airplane was lost. (NJAHOF.)

CLARENCE D. CHAMBERLIN. In 1927, with Acosta as copilot, Clarence D. Chamberlin made an endurance flight of 51 hours, 11 minutes from Roosevelt Field in New York. Chamberlin was an exhibition pilot, barnstormer, test pilot, and a photographic and transport pilot. Chamberlin, called "Mr. Teterboro" in the 1920s and 1930s, was a popular icon at the airport. (NJAHOF.)

AIRPLANE CHANGE. Aron "Duke" Krantz just completed an airplane change in this 1927 photograph. The stunt men and women had to be in excellent physical shape since they were battling strong winds and a bumpy ride in the turbulence. These stunts were always performed without a parachute. If a stunt man missed the ladder or lost his grip in the wind stream, the results were always fatal. (NJAHOF.)

BATTLING A HEADWIND. Capt. Omer Locklear is setting up to change from a Canuck airplane flown by Milton "Skeeter" Elliott to a Canuck flown by Shirley Short. These stunts were dangerous and often fatal to a miscalculating daredevil. The performers on the wings did not wear parachutes, and one slip in a headwind of 65 miles per hour or greater meant certain death. (NJAHOF.)

SOUTHERN CROSS. The Teterboro Fokker-built trimotor *Southern Cross* was the first airplane to cross the Pacific Ocean. On May 31, 1928, Sir Charles Kingsford Smith and crew took off from Oakland, California. The *Southern Cross* landed in Brisbane, Australia, on June 9, where a crowd of 25,000 people waited to greet the *Southern Cross* at the airport. Anthony Fokker sold the airplane for $15,000. (NJAHOF.)

GATES CRASH. Ivan Gates was reportedly flying this aircraft when he crashed it into a swimming pool. The information on the back of the photograph said there was a sign for pool swimmers saying, "No Diving." Gates walked away from this crash, but it is unclear if he parachuted. (NJAHOF.)

CHAMBERLIN'S TRANSATLANTIC AIRPLANE. In 1927, Clarence D. Chamberlin was the second pilot to fly a nonstop transatlantic flight from Roosevelt Field in New York to Eisleben, Germany. He flew 3,911 miles in 42 hours and 31 minutes, a distance longer than Charles A. Lindbergh's. In 1927, he also flew the first ship-to-shore flight to New York City from the deck of the ship S.S. *Leviathan* 120 miles out at sea. (NJAHOF.)

FLIGHT RECORD

FLIGHTS
SOUVENIR

M_____ DATE_____

FLIGHT _New York-Saratoga_ DURATION (APPROX.) 2 HRS. ___ MIN.

The NEW YORKER, in which you flew, is an eight-ten passenger, enclosed cabin Fokker airliner, powered with three Wright *Whirlwind* engines. It is a sister ship to the *Josephine Ford* and *America*, in which Commander BYRD flew over the North Pole and to France; the *Friendship*, in which Miss EARHART flew to England, and the *Southern Cross* of trans-Pacific fame.   The NEW YORKER can stay in the air on any one motor, and has an extended glide, the distance depending upon the altitude, with all motors cut. Landings are made with motors throttled to idling speed, or as if cut.

General Traffic Agent   _Chief Pilot_

NEW YORK AIRWAYS, Inc.

General Offices
100 EAST 42nd ST., NEW YORK, N. Y.
Telephone Caledonia 2363

Operating Base
TETERBORO AIRPORT
Hasbrouck Heights, N. J.

SOUVENIR FLIGHT RECORD. New York Airways was an early charter airline that operated from Teterboro in the mid-1920s. This 1928 souvenir states that the holder flew a two-hour flight on the *New Yorker*, a Fokker trimotor and a sister ship to the *Josephine Ford* and *America*, from Teterboro to Sarasota, New York. Although it describes the airplane as being able to stay in the air on one engine, for technical reasons, that was highly unlikely. (NJAHOF.)

INTERIOR F-VII. The calendar on the bulkhead proclaims the day to be October 12, 1926, and Anthony Fokker is seated on the right. The secretary appears to be typing. Note the wicker chairs and the absence of seat belts. The chairs also appear to be movable. One can see the throttle levers through the window of the cockpit door. (NJAHOF.)

44

FLYING POLICE UNIT. In 1928, Bergen County Police chief Peter Siccardi (far left) formed the first flying police unit in the United States. The airplane was a Fokker, built in Teterboro. Siccardi earned national press coverage when he directed vehicular traffic by semaphore signals while airborne at a Teterboro air show. Several barnstormers earned "special police" titles and assisted in the patrol duties. (NJAHOF.)

CLYDE PANGBORN. Billed as "Upside Down Pangborn," Clyde Pangborn, a handsome, devil-may-care pilot earned the nickname by flying in air shows inverted. He thrilled the audience by flying upside down from 4,000 feet and spiraling to just a few feet from the ground before righting his airplane. In spite of his death-defying stunts, he outlived most of his contemporaries. (NJAHOF.)

AMELIA EARHART. Amelia Earhart first flew the Atlantic Ocean in 1928, as a passenger on a Teterboro-built Fokker trimotor. She was the first woman to fly across the ocean. The pilots were Lu Gordon (left) and Wilmer Stultz. Behind them is the Fokker trimotor *Friendship*, in which they made the trip. (NJAHOF.)

AIR SHOW CRASH. Flying circus pilot Buck Steele died in this crash on February 18, 1928. There were hundreds of fatalities over the barnstorming years. Some newspapers speculated that part of the motivation of some visitors to the air shows was to see such crashes. The Civil Aeronautics Board eventually relented to the demand for strict regulations to curb the accidents. (NJAHOF.)

FOKKER XA-7. This Fokker XA-7, built at Teterboro, was a prototype attack aircraft ordered by the U.S. Army in December 1929. Its first flight was in January 1931. The XA-7 was a two seat, low wing, all-metal monoplane design. It featured a thick, cantilever wing and tunnel radiator. The General Aviation Manufacturing Corporation entered the airplane in a competition held by the army. A Curtiss A-8 won the competition thus ending the development of the XA-7. (NJAHOF.)

FORD TRI-MOTOR. This is a Ford Tri-Motor, photographed at Teterboro airport in 1929. It was Fokker's main competitor. Ford manufactured only 199, and they drew people because of the perceived safety value. The Ford was made of all metal rather than the fabric, wood, and aluminum tubing found on the Fokker trimotors. (NJAHOF.)

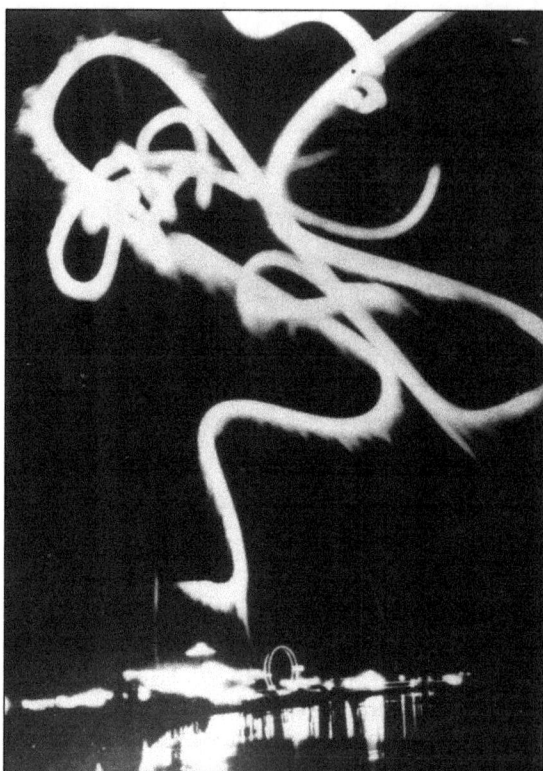

FIREWORKS AT NIGHT. The airplanes of the day were made of mostly wood and fabric. The dope-covered fabric was flammable. Stunt pilots flying these machines who put railroad flares on the wingtips and rear fuselage were pushing the envelope of safety and putting their lives in extreme danger, flying loops and rolls and doing aerobatics. The nighttime show thrilled the crowds, so the show went on. (NJAHOF.)

FOKKER TRIMOTOR F-10, C. 1929. Called the Super Trimotor, the F-10 was an upgraded version of F-VII and was Fokker's first U.S. production trimotor. The 12- to 14-passenger luxury versions had three 425-horsepower Pratt and Whitney Wasp radial engines. Anthony Fokker's plant at Teterboro built 65 F-10 and 59 F-10As. American Airlines, Pan American World Airways, and other airlines operated them. (NJAHOF.)

BENDIX AIRPORT. In 1937, Vincent Bendix bought 100 acres for the site for of Eclipse-Pioneer Division of the Bendix Aviation Corporation. The Bendix plant attracted other business to the airport's sod runways. The *New York Times* reported that by 1941, the two existing hangars had 60 planes, and the field's waiting list could fill an additional hangar. It also described the buildings as "little better than tin barns, and second class garages." (NJAHOF.)

FOKKER F-10A. This Pan Am Fokker F-10A, built in Teterboro, is similar to the Trans World Airlines (TWA) Fokker F-10 that Notre Dame football coach Knute Rockne lost his life in on March 31, 1931, when the wooden wing separated at 600 feet. It was later determined that there were no access panels to inspect the wing root for rotting. The accident ruined the reputation of Anthony Fokker. (Author's collection.)

BARNSTORMERS AND MECHANICS, C. 1930. Barnstormers and mechanics pictured from left to right are (first row) Dick Kowpper, Herb Kunz, Henry Gelewski, Frank Romano, R. E. Sanders, P. L. Clayton, Nick DeSuca, and Al Ernst; (second row) Martin Kruegel Jr., Stan Gusty, Ed Gorski, William Diehl, Bob Golem, Slim West, Jim Craig, Frank Brick, Charles Greger, Ed Smith, and Mac Jansen. Today their memories and accomplishments are enshrined in the New Jersey Aviation Hall of Fame and Museum at Teterboro. (NJAHOF.)

MAIL PILOT AND POSTMASTER. Dean Smith, the airmail pilot in the cockpit of a DH-4 mail airplane, is receiving special mail from postmaster general Harry S. New. Hadley Field became an airmail depot on December 15, 1924. Although Teterboro was closer to Manhattan, the swampy conditions did not encourage the post office to make it a mail depot. The post office used Hadley Field until October 1928, when Newark Airport became the official mail depot. (NJAHOF.)

50

FOKKER F-32. This is an excellent example of the four-engine Fokker F-32, the largest land airplane in the 1930s. The Fokker F-32 luxury airliner made its first flight from Teterboro Airport in 1929. Note the pusher and pull arrangement of the engines, two in one nacelle. (NJAHOF.)

ARON "DUKE" KRANTZ. Aron "Duke" Krantz taught himself to fly at Teterboro Airport in an airplane he built himself. He made over 1,000 performances with the Gates Flying Circus and more than 500 airplane changes. He was one of the highest-paid performers of the day. After the Gates Flying Circus closed, he worked for the New York *Daily News* in the air photography section. He survived for 40 years after the Gates Flying Circus disbanded. (NJAHOF.)

ANTHONY FOKKER. There is no doubt that Anthony Fokker was a genuine aeronautical pioneer. Sir Charles Kingsford Smith, in his book *My Flying Life*, described Fokker: "Anthony Fokker is one of the world's aeronautical geniuses—abrupt to the point of rudeness and apt easily to offend—on closer acquaintance his amazing and lovable personality is revealed. He is a man who enjoys life to the utmost." (NJAHOF.)

F-32. The side of this Western Air Express (WAE) Fokker F-32 says, "Fox Flying House Party, New York to Hollywood." World War I ace Eddie Rickenbacker, vice president of sales for Fokker, arranged for WAE to fly 60 passengers in two F-32s to the West Coast in what he called an aerial house party. Until New York's LaGuardia Airport opened in 1939, "New York" meant landing in New Jersey and taking a bus to New York. (NJAHOF.)

THE SPIDER. This is Fokker at age 20 in the first airplane he built, called the *Spider*. His business partner destroyed it when he flew it into a tree. During World War I, Fokker designed many aircraft for the German army, including the Fokker Dr.I, the triplane made famous by Manfred "Red Baron" von Richthofen. (NJAHOF.)

ANOTHER FLOOD AT TETERBORO. In this 1937 photograph, Edward Gorski is standing in front of his New Standard Aviation Company after a heavy rainstorm at Teterboro Airport. Gorski was a distributor of Aeronca airplanes. Alongside him is an Aeronca C-3 on floats, appropriate for the conditions. In a bit of irony, the Aeronca was nicknamed the flying bathtub because of its physical resemblance to a bathtub. (NJAHOF.)

TROPHY WINNERS, C. 1930. Bill Hartig (left) and Clarence D. Chamberlin congratulate each other. Chamberlin set an altitude record of 19,363 feet. Hartig was a chief mechanic for both Wittemann and Fokker aircraft companies. He then became chief mechanic for Chamberlin, who called him, "the greatest mechanic of the day." (NJAHOF.)

INSIDE THE FOKKER PLANT. The information on this photograph says this is Steve Forberger, a Fokker employee, inspecting an F-32 wing. Notice the sand bags used to leverage the bracing in order to stretch the fabric across the wing. Also note that Forberger is using a chair instead of a ladder. The photograph, dated March 27, 1930, indicates that Forberger died on December 30 of that year in an air accident in Washington, D.C. (NJAHOF.)

54

CHARLES A. AND ANNE MORROW LINDBERGH. In late 1930, Charles A. and Anne Morrow Lindbergh flew their Lockheed *Sirius* into Teterboro Airport to have its engine serviced prior to their spring flight to the Orient. By the spring of 1931, Anne had soloed at Teterboro and earned her radio operator's license. She later wrote *North to the Orient*, describing their adventure. (NJAHOF.)

AERONCA FACE OFF. On the left are five 36-horsepower Aeronca C-3s lined up at the Fokker plant. The airplane had odd lines that earned it the nickname, "the flying bathtub." Facing them are four 1937 Aeronca L low-wing classics. The Aeronca L design reflected greater attention to aerodynamics and included large wheel spats for the fixed gear and a Townend ring for the engine. (NJAHOF.)

RUTH NICHOLS. Ruth Nichols is standing in front of the Lockheed *Vega* in which she set a woman's altitude record of 28,743 feet in 1931. By then, Nichols had established herself in aviation as the cofounder of *Sportsman Pilot* magazine. Nichols was the only woman to hold simultaneous speed, altitude, and distance records for heavy airplanes. Clarence D. Chamberlin was her technical advisor. (NJAHOF.)

BENDIX TROPHY. In 1931, a pilot named Cliff Henderson had an idea for a transcontinental race to attract the best and most daring pilots of the day. He convinced Vincent Bendix to sponsor the race. Bendix gave a $15,000 purse for the race and commissioned a large, art deco, bronze trophy that became the ultimate prize for pilots for decades to come. To promote his new facility at Teterboro, he added a second lap to the race. (NJAHOF.)

FOKKER COLLAGE. Anthony Fokker is at the bottom in this montage, looking up with pride at the famous Fokker aircraft, which achieved daring records and epoch-making flights. In the upper right is the U.S. Army T-2, which, in May 1923, made the first nonstop coast-to-coast flight. Lt. Oakley Kelly and Lt. John MacReady flew from Long Island, New York, to San Diego in 26 hours and 50 minutes. (NJAHOF.)

AIR SHOW FACES, C. 1935. The Gates Flying Circus had shut down, and the government had put strict rules for performers into practice. That, however, did not quell the enthusiasm a decade later when the air show performers were still giving visitors the thrills and excitement of a Teterboro air show. The expressions on these children's faces are universal. (NJAHOF.)

CHAMBERLIN'S CURTISS CONDOR AT TETERBORO. After Clarence D. Chamberlin's record-setting flight across the Atlantic with a passenger in 1927, he formed Chamberlin Airlines, using this Curtiss Condor for service from New York to Boston and points in New England. He carried over half a million passengers, covered over 2 million miles, and chalked up over 20,000 flight hours. (NJAHOF.)

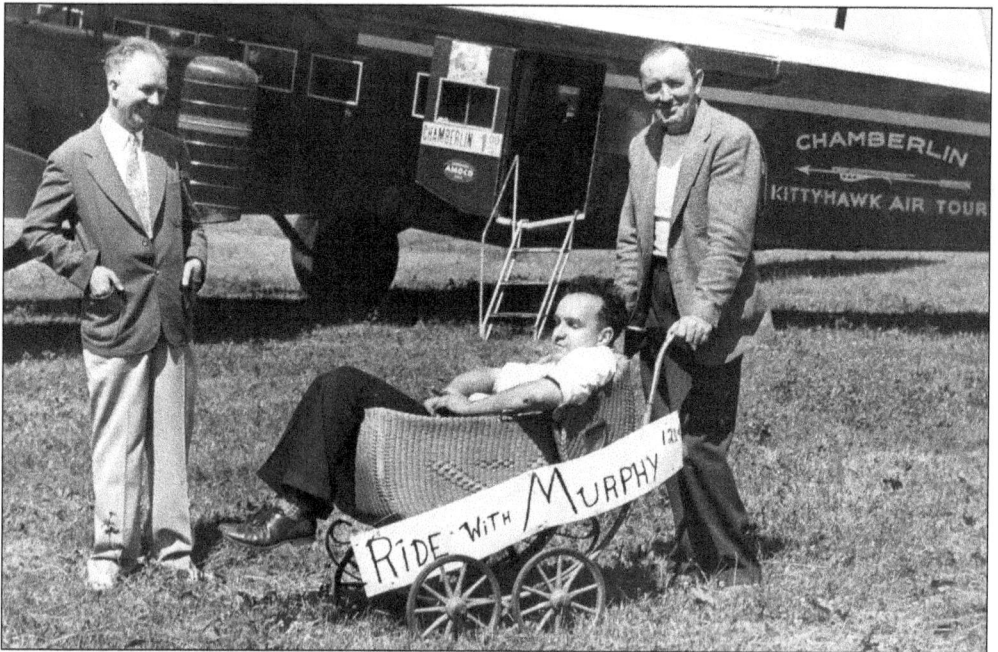

RIDE WITH MURPHY. Chamberlin (left) looks on as a friend pushes a baby carriage with a grown-up advertising "Ride with Murphy" for 12½¢. There is no record to describe what the sign meant or who the adults were. For several years, Chamberlin used four Curtiss Condors to barnstorm the country. Chamberlin charged $1 to $2 for a ride in one. (NJAHOF.)

BENDIX TROPHY RACE, 1934. Vincent Bendix (right) is congratulating Douglas Davis, the winner of the 1934 Bendix race. The airplane was a Wendell Williams racer that achieved an average speed of 216 miles per hour. The last Bendix race was in 1962. AlliedSignal revived the trophy in 1998, as the AlliedSignal Bendix Trophy for Aviation Safety. (NJAHOF.)

JACKIE COCHRAN. A contemporary of Amelia Earhart, Cochran established 75 aviation records from the 1930s to the 1960s, many of them originating or terminating at Teterboro. She earned the prestigious Harmon Trophy five times. In 1938, she won both legs of the Bendix air race, with an average speed of 242 miles per hour. (NJAHOF.)

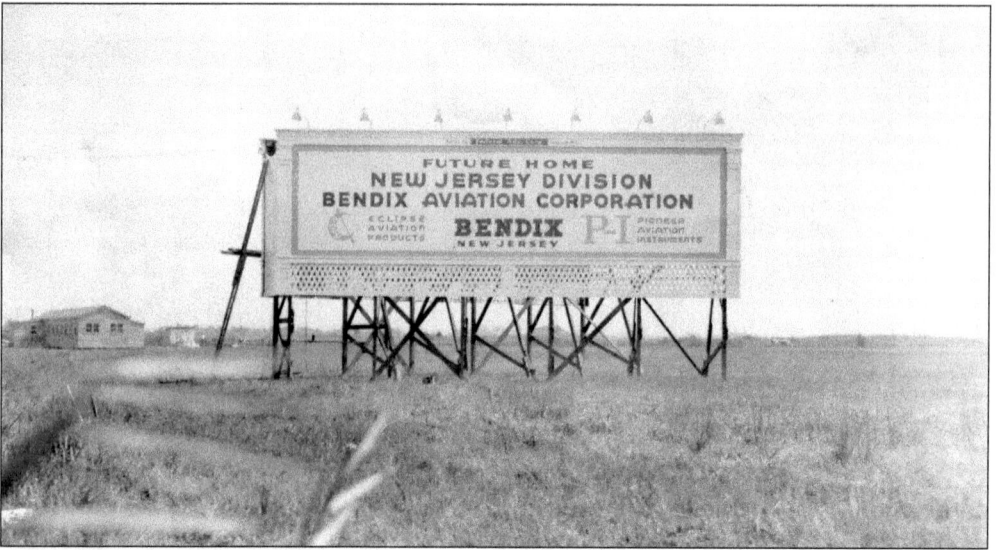

SIGN PROCLAIMING BENDIX, NEW JERSEY. This sign, photographed on August 31, 1937, announced the future home of the New Jersey Division of Bendix Aviation Corporation, which was coming to nearby Hasbrouck Heights. When Bendix purchased 100 acres of land to build a factory, 25 of Teterboro's 26 citizens voted to change the town's and airport's name to Bendix. The factory, a great boost to the local economy, and was not demolished until 2008. (NJAHOF.)

GOODYEAR AIRSHIP LOOKING EAST. During the 1939 New York World's Fair in Flushing, New York, Teterboro Airport became an airship base. The Goodyear airship *Mayflower* made daily sightseeing trips, carrying passengers, the press, city officials, and advertising flights over the fair in New York City and northern New Jersey. The cost of a ride was $5. The *Mayflower*'s "Skytacular" had a colorful array of 1,540 lights per side in red, green, yellow, and blue and was the first Goodyear blimp sign to add moving figures and text. (NJAHOF.)

LOOKING EAST. Taken in the 1940s, this photograph shows little development of the airport and the surrounding community of Hasbrouck Heights. The Fokker factory is on the far right, with the Wright Aeronautical hangar to its left. Runway 6-24 is not yet extended to Route 46, which is on the far left. New York City is in the background. (NJAHOF.)

BRENT BALCHEN. Brent Balchen, a Fokker test pilot, was the first man to fly an airplane over the South Pole as Comdr. Richard E. Byrd's chief pilot in 1929. On the afternoon of May 19, 1932, Amelia Earhart, Balchen, and Ed Gorski departed Teterboro for Harbour Grace, Newfoundland, the starting point for Earhart's solo transatlantic flight. (NJAHOF.)

DR. ALBERT PLESMAN AND ANTHONY FOKKER. After the death of Notre Dame football coach Knute Rockne in one of Fokker's trimotors, Anthony Fokker was no longer the world's foremost aviation innovator. The new name to reckon with was Donald Douglas. Dr. Albert Plesman (left), owner of KLM Royal Dutch Airlines, ordered 10 Douglas DC-2s and used Fokker as his purchasing agent. (Author's collection.)

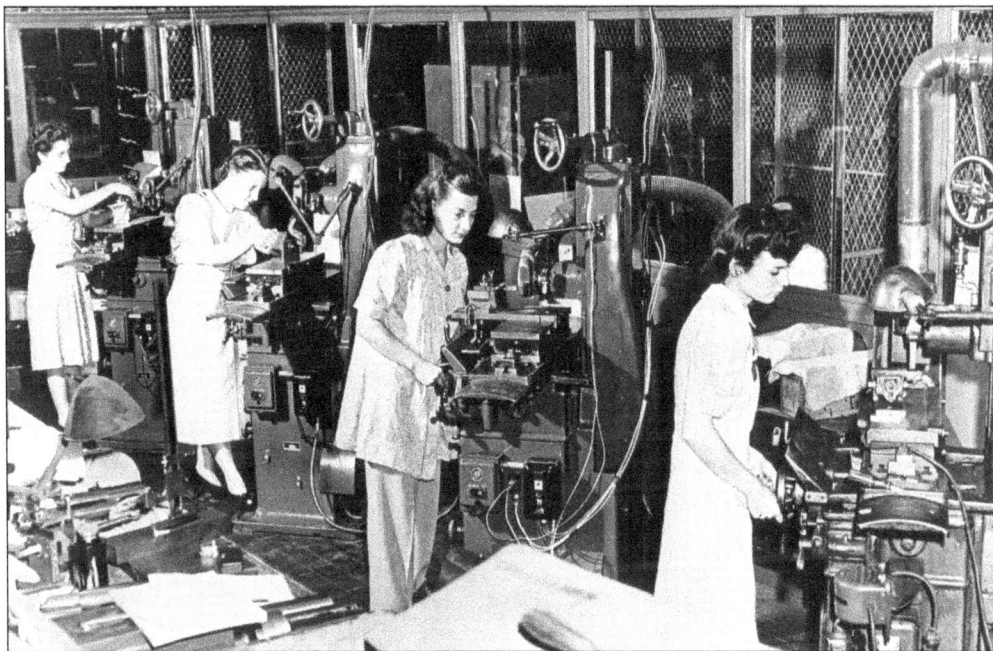

BENDIX FACTORY, WORLD WAR II. On October 10, 1942, the men and women of the Eclipse-Pioneer Division of the Bendix Aviation Corporation, known as "the Invisible Crew," received the prestigious Army-Navy E award for their "exceptional performance on the production front . . . A recognition of the persevering, undaunted, invincible American spirit." (NJAHOF.)

BENDIX MACHINE SHOP, WORLD WAR II. Production at Bendix Aviation Corporation swelled from a monthly sales volume of $625,000 in 1939 to a peak of $30,650,000 in 1945. By the end of 1943, the Eclipse-Pioneer Division and its subcontractors were exceeding a monthly output of 375,000 products, consisting of 70 types of aircraft instrumentation and engine components. (NJAHOF.)

EDWARD GORSKI. Edward Gorski, at age 15, began his aviation career helping Clarence D. Chamberlin build aircraft in an old barn the Wittemann brothers had purchased. In 1924, when Anthony Fokker moved his corporation into the Wittemann plant, Gorski went to work for Fokker as a mechanic. Gorski later started a fixed-base operator (FBO) at Teterboro, which was the first on the East Coast awarded a prewar Civilian Pilot Training Program by the government. (NJAHOF.)

DOUGLAS DC-3. By 1939, 90 percent of U.S. airlines were using Douglas DC-3s. The DC-3 also replaced almost all the Fokker trimotors as a safe and dependable aircraft. This American Airlines DC-3, NC14988, s/n 1494, was the first production model built as a Douglas Sleeper Transport (DST), which carried 21 passengers or 14 sleeper passengers. Converted to a C-49 during the war, it crashed on March 14, 1942, in Knobnoster, Missouri. (NJAHOF.)

BLIMP VIEW. This 1939 aerial view of Teterboro shows the Goodyear airship hangar built for the blimp's appearances at the 1939 New York World's Fair. State Route 46 is behind the hangar. Notice the areas of undeveloped land on both sides of Route 46. Today all the land south of Route 46 where the hangar sits includes runways and taxiways, and the other side of Route 46 has light industry and private homes. (NJOHOF.)

VIEW FROM ABOVE. The former Fokker building is now the Bendix plant and is immediately below in this 1939 photograph taken from the Goodyear blimp *Rainbow*. Route 17 is in the background. It is unknown why there seems to be little activity at the airport in this photograph. (NJOHOF.)

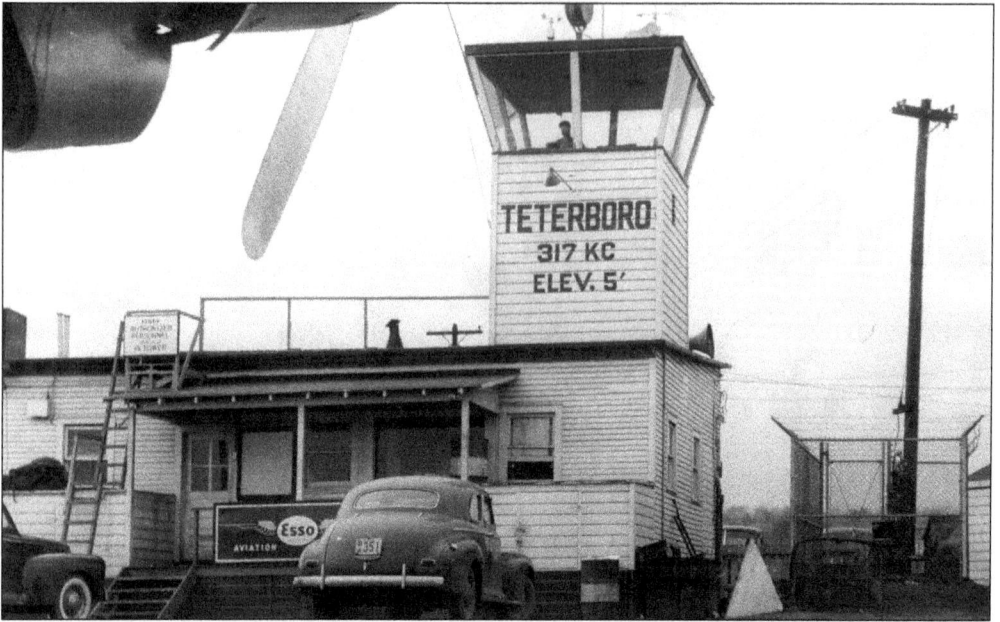

FIRST CONTROL TOWER, C. 1946. Note the field elevation of five feet and the tower frequency. This was the operations building without the tower cab. George Hicha stood on the roof of the building and used a light gun to signal the aircraft. A cab, added to the roof in late 1946, provided him shelter in bad weather. This building was located alongside the Atlantic Aviation Corporation hangar. (NJAHOF.)

GEORGE HICHA. Hicha was the only air-traffic controller employed by Fred Wehran in 1946 to control air traffic. He worked traffic from sunrise to sunset. When Hicha began the job, the field covered 500 acres and had one 3,000-foot sod runway. This tower was the first air-traffic control tower on the field. Just below Hicha is a Willis Air Service DC-3. (NJAHOF.)

Two

POSTWAR TETERBORO
1946–1964

OLD CONTROL TOWER. The airport manager moved the tower cab to the junction of the runways and mounted it on a wooden framework. By late 1947, the field had three paved runways. Two of them, 6-24 and 1-19, were 4,500-feet long by 100-feet wide, running north–south. An 80-foot runway (32) ran east–west. According to H. V. "Pat" Reilly in his book _From the Balloon to the Moon_, Hicha, the airport's first controller, was handling 1,200 movements a day, and Teterboro ranked the ninth-busiest airport in the nation. (NJAHOF.)

CONTROL TOWER UNDER CONSTRUCTION, C. 1946. The first permanent control tower is under construction beside the Atlantic Aviation Corporation hangar. The U.S. Army Airforce delivered this hangar in pieces and reassembled it on site. An extension to the hangar was built, and the tower attached to the extension on the right corner. (NJAHOF.)

ATLAS SKY MERCHANT. In 1946, the Atlas Supply Company hired Col. Edwin E. Aldrin to purchase a war surplus C-54 and create a flying showroom to display Atlas tires, batteries, and accessories. Aldrin and his team flew the Atlas Sky Merchant around the world. The flight, the first of its kind, originated in Miami and terminated at Teterboro. The 100-day flight covered 44,500 miles. (NJAHOF.)

FIREFIGHTERS AT TETERBORO. The Teterboro control tower is under construction in this photograph from about 1947. Behind the fire truck is NC58022, a Kansas City Southern Skyways's DC-3. This was one of dozens of tramp airlines that trolled the skies as nonscheduled airlines and air freighters after the war. The fire truck carries the name Teterboro Air Terminal, the name used while Fred Wehran owned the airport. (NJAHOF.)

EXPERIMENTAL TURBOPROP. In 1946, three B-17Gs that used Curtiss Wright Cyclone engines were modified as flying test beds for experimental turboprop engines. The first conversion, seen here, was turned over to the Wright Aeronautical Company at Teterboro. The aircraft was fitted with a 5,500-horsepower Wright XT35 Typhoon turboprop in the nose. The engine was ultimately unsuccessful and did not go into production. (NJAHOF.)

69

GENE AUTRY. Teterboro Airport had many famous people arriving and departing over the years, among them Gene Autry, pictured here in 1947. Pres. Richard Nixon, Pres. Gerald R. Ford, Vice Pres. Walter Mondale, Vice Pres. George Bush, Prince Bernhard of the Netherlands, golfer Arnold Palmer, and entertainers Bill Cullen and Johnny Carson were some of the visiting celebrities. (NJAHOF.)

TETERBORO AIRPORT, WINTER 1947. Royal French Rider (left) and Mike Bachik were test pilots who worked for the Bendix Aviation Corporation. Behind them is an ice covered, converted B-25 bomber. The ship was used to test flight instruments, among them the Bendix PB-10 autopilot. (NJAHOF.)

FRANK BRICK. Before World War II, Frank Brick was vice president and chief engineer of Finch Telecommunications. He helped develop the company's secret electronic equipment for the government, including radar. He tested the products in a Fokker Super Universal. During World War II, he served as an officer in the Bendix Civil Air Patrol (CAP) stationed at Teterboro. He later commanded CAP Group 221 at Teterboro. (NJAHOF.)

GROWING AIRPORT. By 1947, three hard surface runways replaced the original sod runway, and there were vast areas of taxiways and other facilities of a modern airport. There were 400 to 500 aircraft of all categories on the field. Pictured here is Atlantic Aviation Corporation hangar No. 1. The runways are just beyond in the upper right of the photograph, and Industrial Avenue is on the left. (NJAHOF.)

POSTWAR TETERBORO. By July 1947, more than 1,000 veterans developed Teterboro Airport from a field that handled 50 movements a day at the end of the war into an operation involving 1,000 a day. Veterans transformed the airport from a gaggle of tents to metal Nissan huts and large, modern metal hangars. In 1949, *Aero Digest* magazine said Teterboro was "the busiest privately-owned air freight terminal in the world." (NJAHOF.)

BOMBSHELL ROUND-THE-WORLD FLYER. In April 1947, William Odom flew this Teterboro-modified A-26 Invader around the world. *Bombshell* established a record time of 78 hours, 55 minutes, surpassing by 12 hours the record set by Howard Hughes in 1938. The flight originated and terminated in Chicago. This airframe was converted to pressurized executive configuration by Grand Central Aircraft in Glendale, California, between 1952 and 1953 and registered N4852Y. (NJAHOF.)

FIRST LIGHT AIRPLANE ROUND-THE-WORLD FLIGHTS. In 1947, pilot Clifford Evans, flying *City of Washington* (NX2365M), and George Truman, flying *City of Los Angeles* (NX3671M) flew around the world. Evans and Truman prepared the two Piper Cub Super Cruisers for the four-month trip at the Safair FBO at Teterboro. Today NX2365M hangs in the National Air and Space Museum, in Washington, D.C. (Author's collection.)

CONTROL TOWER VIEW. This 1948 photograph shows the air-traffic controllers operating very basic equipment. Bertram Schram, the operator standing up, is using a light-signaling device, an instrument that harkened back to the 1930s. Seated are Chris Rauscher, chief control officer (left), and Dan Kaplan, assistant control officer. Across the field is the future home of the current control tower and the New Jersey Aviation Hall of Fame and Museum. (NJAHOF.)

CONTROL TOWER. "MAC," on the side of the helicopter (NC115B), stands for Metropolitan Aviation Corporation, one of the first passenger helicopter services in America based at Teterboro. The two-seat Model 47B, the first commercial evolution of Bell's pioneering Model 30, is passing the first control tower at the intersecting runways 6-24 and 1-19. (NJAHOF.)

BENDIX PLANT, NOVEMBER 1948. After World War II, Teterboro suffered heavily from the cancellation of contracts, subcontractors, and government facilities closing. Bendix Aviation Corporation management decided not to rely on military sales. Instead, it began to develop commercial aviation products. This work included autopilots, flight-path controls, oxygen regulators, and turbine starters for the commercial air-transport market. Route 17 is in the background. (NJAHOF.)

SANTA ARRIVES. The annual arrival of Santa via a Bell 47B helicopter, seen here in 1948, is a longtime practice. Usually Santa left the North Pole a week or so before Christmas Eve and arrived at the airport on a Saturday morning. He circled a few times so the children could wave, then he landed to meet and greet them. The practice continues today. (NJAHOF.)

AERIAL VIEW OF THE TOWER. The 80-foot tower opened in 1948; it was built for an estimated $250,000. At the time, its instrument landing equipment was said to put Teterboro on a par with major air terminals in the nation and believed it would help relieve much of the postwar air-traffic congestion. The new system allowed aircraft to pick up glide-path signals from a 15-mile radius. (NJAHOF.)

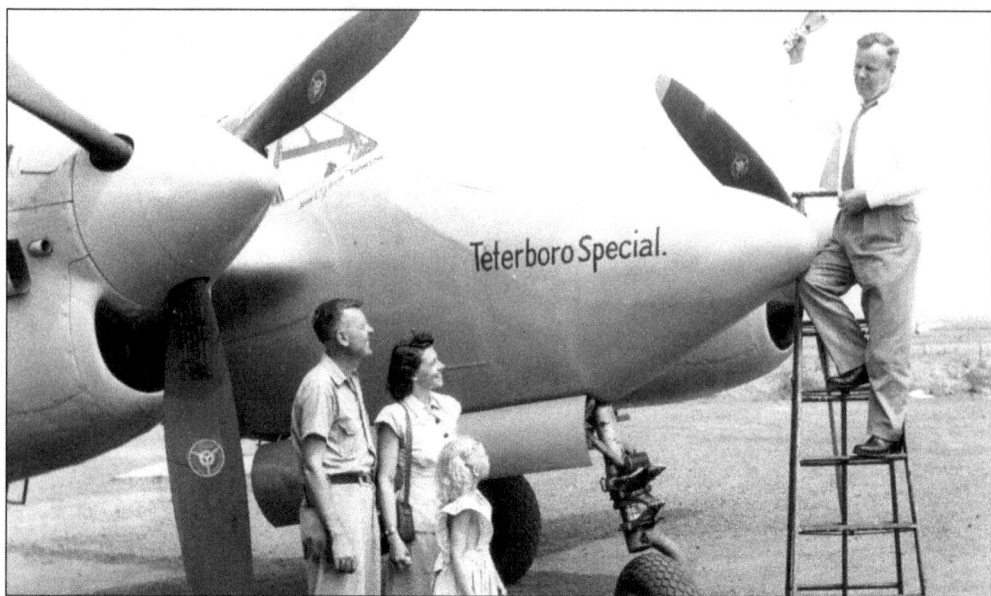

FRED L. WEHRAN. Fred L. Wehran is christening race pilot John Thompson's P-38, as Thompson's family looks on. Wehran saw the possibility to develop Teterboro Airport into a thriving commercial enterprise. Its nearness to New York City was a perfect location for an airfreight operation. In 1939, Wehran purchased it for $50,000 and saved it from becoming an industrial park. Wehran sold the airport to the Port Authority of New York in 1949 for $3.2 million. (NJAHOF.)

WILLIAM ODOM. From March 6–8, 1949, William Odom flew the *Waikiki Beech* across the Pacific from Hawaii to California then on to Teterboro Airport. He flew 5,273 miles in just over 36 hours, while burning only 272 gallons of fuel. The feat earned Odom a place in aviation history; however, he died in a racing accident later that year. (NJAHOF.)

GOODYEAR GA-2 DUCK. This Goodyear GA-2 Duck (NC5500M) is over the Atlantic Aviation Corporation hangar at Teterboro Airport. Only 16 Goodyear GA-2s were built in 1947. Although the design was solid, the escalating costs pushed the price tag up and eliminated it from the personal airplane market. All 16 became demonstrator aircraft. Another Duck sits on the ramp below. (NJAHOF.)

ROYAL FRENCH RYDER. Bendix Aviation Corporation test pilot Royal French Ryder is standing in front of the North American F-82 Twin Mustang. In 1947, the newly formed U.S. Air Force Strategic Air Command employed F-6 Mustangs and F-82 Twin Mustangs due to their range capabilities. Ryder tested Bendix flight instruments of all types, including the Bendix automatic approach and landing systems. (NJAHOF.)

NORTH AMERICAN F-82 TWIN MUSTANG. Here is U.S. Air Force 465162, a Twin Mustang running up in front of the Bendix hangar at Teterboro Airport. This long range, all-weather fighter served at McGuire Air Force Base in New Jersey from October 4, 1949, through 1950, and was probably at Bendix for flight-instrument modifications. This aircraft is undergoing restoration at the National Museum of the United States Air Force for static display. (NJAHOF.)

WINTER MAINTENANCE. This Flota Aérea Mercante Argentina (FAMA) DC-4 is undergoing engine maintenance in a makeshift lean-to after a snowstorm at Teterboro Airport. Although it has windows, it is unlikely it served as a passenger airliner, and more likely, it was a freight dog. It was passed to the nationalized Aerolineas Argentinas in 1949 and named *Tte Origine*. The aircraft was withdrawn from use in 1970. (NJAHOF)

BEECHCRAFT STAGGERWING. This photograph, taken prior to 1949, shows a Beechcraft Model F-17D Staggerwing nosed over at Teterboro. It is likely that the airplane was hit by a strong tailwind after touchdown. This airplane was produced in 1938 and impressed by U.S. Air Force in 1942 as UC-43C. It returned on the civil register as NC46296. (NJAHOF.)

TETERBORO AFTER WORLD WAR II. This post–World War II photograph shows a section of Teterboro Airport where the old Fokker/Wittemann building was located. Notice the roof no longer sports the Bendix name. It is now surrounded by an assortment of general-aviation aircraft and smaller hangars and workshops. Runway 6-24 is in the background. (NJAHOF.)

NEWARK AIRPORT, C. 1949. The administration building is being used as a terminal and was overwhelmed with passenger and air traffic after World War II. Ownership by the port authority allowed Newark to develop into a thriving airport while Teterboro languished. When the port authority took over Teterboro Airport, it began to make millions of dollars in infrastructure improvements. (NJAHOF.)

TEXACO'S EXECUTIVE AIRCRAFT. The Convair CV-240 series and its variants were produced from 1947 through 1956. Approximately 125 were manufactured for the airlines. This aircraft served Texaco at Teterboro Airport as N1620. It was later sold and reregistered as N90851 to Mission Air Lift because Texaco recycled its N numbers to succeeding airplanes. (NJAHOF.)

HURRICANE, C. 1951. This is Marjorie Gray Aero Services's tie-down area after a hurricane rolled through in the early 1950s. In those years, private flying was very popular and hangar space limited. The owners of these three airplanes and others on the field learned a costly lesson: evacuate before the hurricane hits or get the airplane inside a sturdy building. (NJAHOF.)

WRIGHT-BELLANCA MONOPLANE. Bernard McFadden, a publisher and physical culturist, owned this Wright-Bellanca monoplane named for his magazine *Miss True Story*, one of his better-known publications. McFadden inspired millions of people around the world to live healthful and vigorous lives. At the peak of his career, he owned several hotels and a major building in New York City. (NJAHOF.)

81

KATHERINE MENGES BRICK. Katherine Menges "Kay" Brick was a member of the Women Airforce Service Pilots (WASP) in 1943 and flew as a ferry command pilot. After the war, she became the executive director of the All Women's Transcontinental Air Race (Powder Puff Derby). Brick established that organization's national headquarters in Safair's FBO at Teterboro Airport, and she held the position of executive director for 14 years. (NJAHOF.)

BENDIX B-25. Bendix Aviation Corporation at Teterboro Airport used this World War II surplus B-25 for flight-testing avionics. Bendix (later Honeywell International) was a key aircraft parts manufacturing site during World War II. Honeywell International shut down its underused aviation manufacturing plant in Teterboro in 2008. The hangar was located off Malcolm and Industrial Avenues. (NJAHOF.)

LOCKHEED 18-LODESTAR. This Lockheed Lodestar N25601 is in private ownership in this late-1940s photograph at Teterboro. The first deliveries of this type were made to Mid-Continent Airlines in March 1940, but the bulk of production was for the U.S. Army Air Force. The type found ready acceptance as a business aircraft after World War II, and there were several conversions by private companies. (NJAHOF.)

TETERBORO GROWING. This postwar photograph shows Atlantic Aviation Corporation hangar No. 3, with a mix of aircraft. To the upper right of the hangar are some of the temporary Nissan huts set up after the war to house the businesses the returning veterans were starting. Notice the all-black Convair CV 330 (N8420H) below in private ownership. (NJAHOF.)

DC-3 Engine Work. For years, Teterboro Airport lacked adequate hangar space for winter maintenance. Here five mechanics are working outside in the weather on a Douglas DC-3 not long after a snowfall. While in private ownership, Teterboro could not afford the millions of dollars needed to upgrade its infrastructure to bring it up to the standards of the Newark Airport. (NJAHOF.)

Marjorie Gray. Marjorie Gray served over two years in the Women's Auxiliary Ferry Squadron of the Air Transport Command. She flew 19 different types of aircraft, from the Piper Cub through the C-47 to the heavy B-25 bomber. After World War II, she opened a FBO at Teterboro Airport. (NJAHOF.)

TETERBORO AIRPORT, C. 1950. Gray's FBO was tucked into the southwest corner of the airport off Industrial Avenue. She was one of the first women in the United States to open an FBO. She operated the facility from 1946 to 1951. The airplanes would have to taxi across Industrial Avenue to gain access to the runways. Today this area is the site of a water-pumping station. (NJAHOF.)

B-18 BOLO BOMBER. The Douglas Aircraft Company developed the B-18 based on the Douglas DC-2 airframe to replace the Martin B-10 as the U.S. Army Air Corps's standard bomber. During World War II, every American military aircraft including this B-18 contained one or more of the 70 basic types of aircraft instrumentation or engine components made by the Bendix Aviation Corporation Teterboro facility. (NJAHOF.)

CURTISS COMMANDO C-46. Meteor Air Transport, based at Teterboro Airport, was a charter company that operated contracts to fly passengers to U.S. destinations, Europe, and other parts of the world. At one point, Meteor Air Transport had 12 airframes, four former C-46 Curtiss Commandos, six former C-47s, and two former C-54s. (NJAHOF.)

DOUGLAS B-23 DRAGON. Postwar aviation was booming in the United States in the late 1940s. This corporate aircraft is a former Douglas B-23 Dragon bomber, based on the Douglas DC-3 airframe. It was the first operational U.S. bomber equipped with a tail gun position. It first flew on July 27, 1939. After World War II, when corporations were looking for airplanes for their executives, they found this an ideal airframe. (NJAHOF.)

HISTORY-MAKING PILOTS, C. 1955. From left to right are Clarence D. Chamberlin, Ruth Nichols, and Blanch Scott. In 1910, Scott was the first American woman to solo an airplane, and Nichols flew with Chamberlin on the first midnight flight to Chicago to deliver newspapers. Chamberlin was the second man to solo across the Atlantic and the first to carry a passenger. (NJAHOF.)

MORE FLOODING. This postwar photograph shows an assortment of ex-C-47s and C-54s awaiting cargo and passengers at the Willis Air Service and Safir FBOs. Note the semi-flooded field from melting snow. Off in the distance in the upper right is the old Wittemann/Fokker factory building. The roadway on the right is Industrial Avenue. (NJAHOF.)

METEOR AIR TRANSPORT. The Meteor Air Transport hangar off Industrial Avenue appears to be doing a booming business in this postwar photograph, judging from the packed parking lots. Visible are three former Curtiss C-46s and two C-54s. Industrial Avenue is to the right of the hangar. (NJAHOF.)

TETERBORO PASSENGER LOUNGE, LATE 1940s. This staged photograph illustrated the comfort that awaited the passengers using the Teterboro Airport terminal. Looking east is New York's Empire State Building. The man is reading an aviation magazine featuring a story titled the "New Beechcraft G17S." The G17S Staggerwing was an enclosed biplane that came along in 1946, dating this photograph to soon after that period. (NJAHOF.)

ATLANTIC AVIATION MACHINE SHOP CREW. This undated photograph shows Atlantic Aviation Corporation mechanics at work. The Brewster Aeronautical Company built the largest Atlantic Aviation hangar, and Atlantic Aviation had a large FBO in it that continues to this day. As jets came on the scene, its business increased. (NJAHOF.)

HANGAR FIRE, JUNE 10, 1948. This Stinson 108 NC40101 was destroyed along with 50 other aircraft belonging to the Safair and Rausch Flying Services when a fire gutted two large hangars. According to the *New York Times*, the fire started when a leaking airplane fuel tank exploded. The total damage was over a half-million dollars. (NJAHOF.)

TETERBORO FIRE TRUCK. This is one of the fire trucks that responded to the 1948 fire (note the charred remains). Today a "99 to heights" call has the Hasbrouck Heights Fire Department responding to Teterboro Airport. It is the fire command for the airport. Any accident or airport fire today will have Hackensack, Moonachie, Lodi, the port authority, and other neighboring fire departments responding as needed. (NJAHOF.)

WILLIAM (BILL) RHODE. William (Bill) Rhode washed Gates biplanes and ran errands. He began his parachute-jumping career at Teterboro Airport in 1936. When Rhode broke his back in a parachuting accident in 1945, it marked the end of his jumping career. In 1951, after a period of recuperation and therapy, he began a long career as a flight instructor. When he retired, his logbook showed 32,901 hours. (NJAHOF.)

MICHAEL BACHIK JR. Michael Bachik Jr., a Bendix Aviation Corporation test pilot, helped develop and flight test the first electronic autopilot and flight-path control systems. With Royal French Ryder in a B-25-J, he completed the first Category III hands-off landing at the FAA-National Aviation Facilities Experimental Center in Atlantic City. Today the facility is the William J. Hughes Technical Center. (NJAHOF.)

THE OLD REDHEAD. Known as "the Old Redhead" because of his tea-colored hair, Arthur Godfrey based his private aircraft, this DC-3, at Teterboro Airport. In 1966, Godfrey set a round-the-world record of 86 hours in a Jet Commander. After going through several owners, his DC-3 eventually wound up derelict in South Florida, abandoned by drug smugglers. (Author's collection.)

91

ARTHUR GODFREY BUZZES THE TOWER. In 1954, the FAA accused Arthur Godfrey of purposely buzzing the control tower at Teterboro Airport while taking off in his DC-3. Godfrey claimed the windy conditions required him to turn immediately after takeoff. In fact, he was annoyed because the tower did not give him the runway directly into the wind. Later found guilty, Godfrey had his pilot's license suspended for six months. (Author's collection.)

TETERBORO SCHOOL OF AERONAUTICS. The Teterboro School of Aeronautics is located on the south end of Teterboro Airport off Moonachie Avenue. Charles F. Willis Jr. also founded Willis Air Service, and Teterboro's largest multiengine maintenance facility founded it in 1947. Today it runs full-time programs for airframe and power plant licenses. (NJAHOF.)

AERIAL PHOTOGRAPH. An early-1960s photograph of Teterboro Airport shows large tracts of undeveloped land to the southeast. Industrial Avenue and runway 1-19 are in the foreground. The Bendix Aviation Corporation factory is in the center foreground. The intersecting runway 6-24 in the background has not yet been extended. By the 1970s, the woods and trees in the distance began yielding to housing and light industry. (NJAHOF.)

ANOTHER AERIAL VIEW. Seen around 1960, the neighborhood is slowly edging toward the airfield. Runway 1 was later extended to accommodate the arrival of the jet age, and runway 32 (still active in this photograph) was shut down to become taxiway Foxtrot. It was later redesignated taxiway Golf. Runway 24 (far right center) was later extended to the left to the edge of Route 46. (NJAHOF.)

FLYING TIGER C-47. Fueling is underway on this Flying Tiger's C-47 in front of the Willis Air Service. The Willis Air Service hangar, built after World War II, was the first major structure built at Teterboro Airport since the 1920s. Willis went on to create the Teterboro School of Aeronautics. In 1948, Willis and the Flying Tigers were among the top-five air freight carriers in the United States. (NJAHOF.)

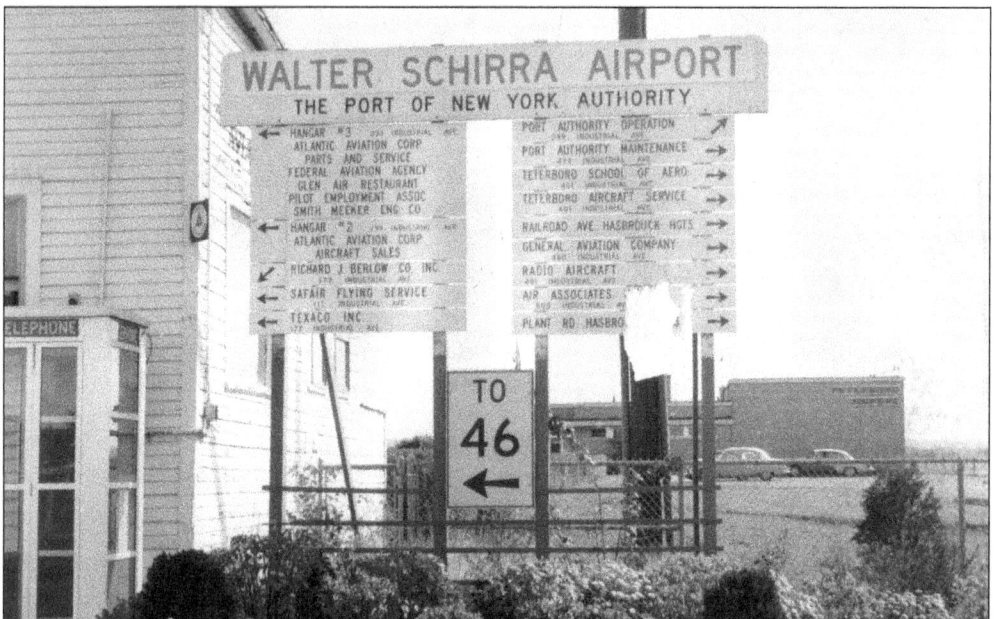

WALTER SCHIRRA AIRPORT. In 1962, Walter Schirra flew a Mercury spacecraft, which he named *Sigma 7*, on a six-orbit flight around the earth. In 1965, as commander of *Gemini 6*, he performed the first rendezvous in orbit with another spacecraft, *Gemini 7*. Schirra was born and raised in New Jersey and bicycled from his home in Oradell to nearby Teterboro Airport. The airport temporarily held his name in honor of his accomplishments. (NJAHOF.)

AIR SHOW CELEBRATION. Dignitaries gather on April 3, 1962, to celebrate an air show. From left to right are Roy S. Samuals, assistant airport manager; Aubrey Keefe, vice president of Texaco; Aron "Duke" Krantz, assistant chief pilot for Bendix Aviation Corporation; Bernt Blachen; Arctic explorer; Royal French Ryder; William Diehl, the first man to land at Teterboro Airport; and Teterboro chief of police Fred Bollander. (NJAHOF.)

TETERBORO AIRPORT, C. 1951. This photograph shows a former C-46 (left) and six former C-47s. There are several smaller airplanes in the foreground that may be military trainers, such as the SNJ. In the upper right is the old Fokker factory without the water tower. Behind it is Malcolm Avenue, and in the upper left is Route 17. Industrial Avenue is in the front of the Fokker building. (NJAHOF.)

BENDIX DC-3. During the 1950s and 1960s, Bendix Aviation Corporation had several aircraft, including this DC-3 N45399. Bendix aircraft were corporate owned (or on loan from the military) and assigned to the various divisions as the need arose. Fitted with experimental radars, the aircraft were instrumental in the development of the Bendix Doppler radar navigation system. The Doppler navigation system also became standard equipment on many commercial and civil aircraft. (NJAHOF.)

AERIAL VIEW OF POSTWAR TETERBORO. In this photograph, runway 32 in the upper right is still operational. Looking east are vast amounts of undeveloped land. By the 1960s, housing and light industry began to encroach on the airport, and runway 32 was closed for safety reasons. The Atlantic Aviation Corporation hangar is completed along with the first control tower. (NJAHOF.)

CHICAGO SOUTHERN DC-4. In 1947, the Eclipse-Pioneer Division of the Bendix Aviation Corporation manufactured and installed the PB-10, an electronic autopilot in this DC-4. It became the first autopilot used on scheduled passenger service. It ultimately received worldwide acceptance, and by 1950, the PB-10 was in use by 24 airlines, including United Airlines, Northwest Airlines, TWA, Delta Air Lines, British Overseas Airways Corporation (BOAC), and Air France. (NJAHOF.)

BENDIX PLANT. On October 24, 1938, Teterboro Airport became the home of the Bendix Aviation Corporation. This move brought both the workers of the Eclipse Machine Company and Pioneer Instruments together under one roof since the acquisition of both companies in 1929. Shortly after moving, war production orders began rolling in from France and England. When America entered World War II in 1941, Bendix was one of the few companies able to fill the U.S. military production orders immediately. (NJAHOF.)

PILOT'S JAMBOREE, JUNE 12, 1965. From left to right are Dean Smith, Herb Fisher, Russ Brinkley, Charles Wittemann (speaking), and William Diehl. Before the annual New Jersey Aviation Hall of Fame and Museum dinner and induction ceremony was established, the legendary pilots of Teterboro got together in what they called the Teterboro Airport Pilot's Jamboree, honoring the early aviators and old-timers. (H. V. Reilly/NJAHOF.)

GLIDE MOBILE. Clarence D. Chamberlin and "Miss MAC," enjoy a ride on the Glide Mobile, built by Charles Fletcher of Sparta. It was the first air-cushioned vehicle in the United States flown successfully. Fletcher hoped he could sell it to the military, but the vehicle was not produced commercially. (H. V. Reilly/NJAHOF.)

Three

THE JET AGE
1965–2009

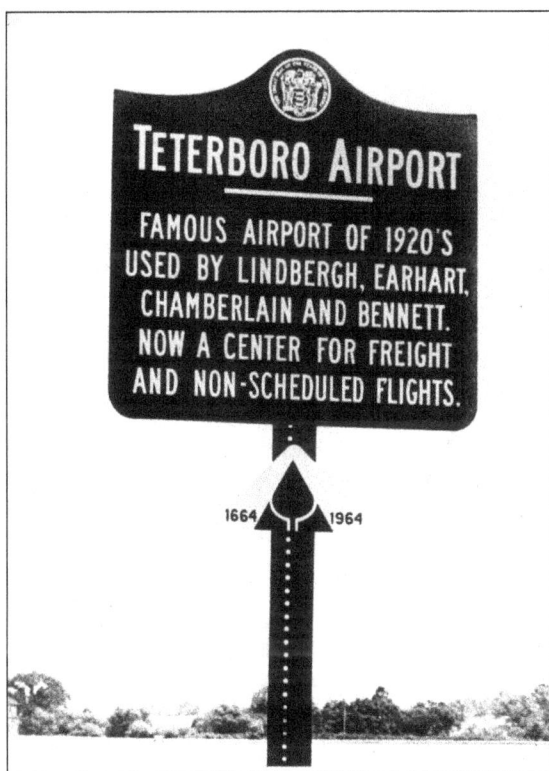

THE 300-YEAR ANNIVERSARY OF TETERBORO. In 1664, Dutch settlers burned the swampy meadowlands for crops. More than 300 years later, the land gave way to a sod airfield. Almost 90 years ago, in 1926, Adm. Richard E. Byrd flew Teterboro-built Fokker trimotors over the North Pole and the Atlantic; Amelia Earhart flew as a passenger over the Atlantic. Clarence Chamberlin, Ruth Nichols, Floyd Bennett, and Charles A. Lindbergh also flew from Teterboro Airport. Teterboro continues to be a busy general-aviation airport. (NJAHOF.)

ATLANTIC AVIATION CORPORATION. In 1946, the Atlantic Aviation Corporation moved a branch of its company, located in Wilmington, Delaware, into Teterboro Airport's west side. The moved allowed it to become the largest FBO on the field. Many notable people have crossed the Atlantic Aviation ramp, including Arnold Palmer, Johnny Carson, and Arthur Godfrey. (NJAHOF.)

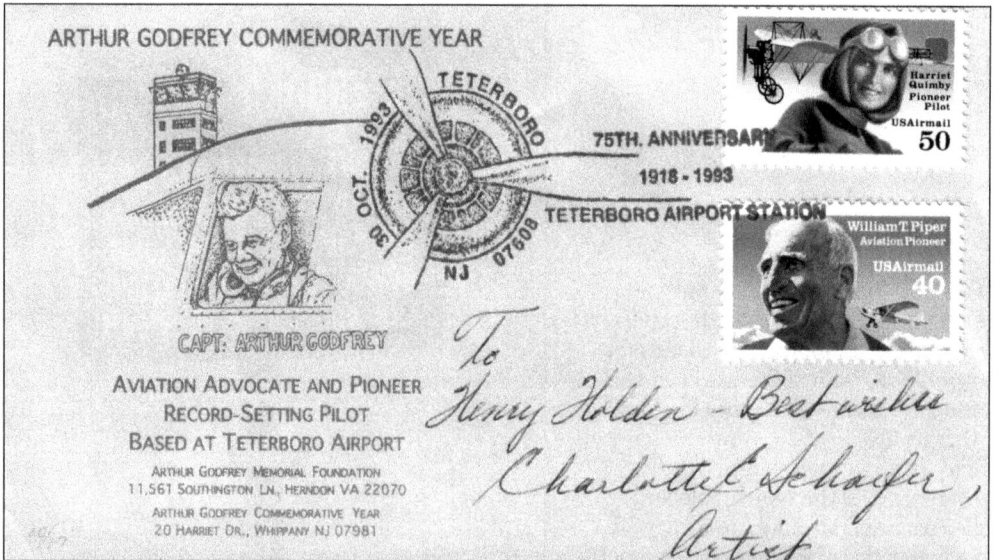

ARTHUR GODFREY COMMEMORATIVE CACHE. Arthur Godfrey learned to fly in the 1930s while doing a radio show in the Washington, D.C., area. Badly injured in a traffic accident on his way to a flying lesson in 1931, Godfrey spent months recuperating, and the injury kept him from flying on active duty during World War II. He served as a reserve officer in the U.S. Navy in a public affairs role. (Author's collection.)

VINTAGE AIRPLANE AND CARS. This photograph shows a DC-3 alongside the Atlantic Aviation Corporation hangar. The control tower was retired in the 1970s and part of it became the Aviation Hall of Fame and Museum at Teterboro. A governor's proclamation on July 3, 1979, changed the name to the New Jersey Aviation Hall of Fame and Museum. Note the vintage cars beneath the control tower. (NJAHOF.)

CLARENCE D. CHAMBERLIN. Standing beneath the control tower, Clarence D. Chamberlin (center), Teterboro pioneer and second man to fly nonstop across the Atlantic in 1927, returned to the field to celebrate Teterboro Airport's 50th anniversary. Flanking him are Capt. O. J. Studman (right), vice president of Pan Am's Metropolitan Air Facilities Division, and R. G. Smith, airport manager. (H. V. Reilly/NJAHOF.)

BENDIX WHITE ROOM, C. 1960S. The space age was the next challenge for Bendix Aviation Corporation at Teterboro Airport. Its Eclipse-Pioneer Division provided the inertial guidance system for the army's solid propellant Pershing Missile program. In 1958, work began on an ultra clean "white room" to produce these products. This program lasted until 1981, when the last production order was shipped. (NJAHOF.)

WALTER SCHIRRA. Walter Schirra learned to fly at Teterboro Airport. Schirra took his first airplane lesson with William Diehl in the 1940s. Schirra is sitting on top of his Mercury 8 space capsule *Sigma 7* in 1968. He was the only person to fly in all of America's first three space programs, Mercury, Gemini, and Apollo. (NASA/NJAHOF.)

PAN AM. In 1970, the port authority leased the airport for 30 years to Pan Am. Within three years, Pan Am had lengthened the runways and constructed four modern hangars at the south end of the field, which developed into an executive office complex that is today the location of Jet Aviation. In 1989, Pan Am sold the operational rights on the remainder of the lease to Johnson Controls. (H. V. Reilly/NJAHOF.)

THE 50TH ANNIVERSARY. More than 500 persons gathered to celebrate the airport's 50th anniversary on August 14, 1970. Among the state, county, and local officials lauding the aviation pioneers of the 1920s were honored guests, from left to right, Aron "Duke" Krantz, Clarence D. Chamberlin, William Diehl, Blanche Noyes, and Royal French Ryder. Bergen County deputy freeholder Frank Bruno (second from right) and Moonachie mayor Dominic Casamassina (right) were also part of the celebration. (H. V. Reilly/NJAHOF.)

HALL OF FAME INDUCTEES ARON "DUKE" KRANTZ AND ARTHUR GODFREY. Teterboro Airport has a rich aviation history; at one time, it was home to the airplanes of record-setting aviators. Long before it became a viable airport, television personality Arthur Godfrey (right) ice-skated and crabbed in the Teterboro meadows. Aron "Duke" Krantz was one of the most famous stuntmen who flew with the Gates Flying Circus. (H. V. Reilly/NJAHOF.)

PAN AM TAKES OVER. At one minute past midnight on January 1, 1970, the Port Authority of New York and New Jersey, handed over the management of Teterboro Airport to Pan Am's Metropolitan Air Facilities Division. Representatives of Pan Am gather in the conference room to celebrate. Johnson Controls later leased the airport, and on December 1, 2000, the port authority assumed full responsibility for operations. (H. V. Reilly/NJAHOF.)

MORE HALL OF FAME INDUCTEES. From left to right are Benjamin Rock (standing) and hall of fame inductees Edward Gorski, William Diehl, and Clarence D. Chamberlin. The three men holding their plaques were inducted into the hall of fame at the first induction dinner in 1973. Rock was inducted six years later. (H. V. Reilly/NJAHOF.)

CONTROL TOWER. In 1973, Teterboro Airport voluntarily applied for and received a certification for safety under part 139 of FAA regulations. It became the first general-aviation airport in the nation to have this certification. Under the regulations, the airport operator must meet the FAA-prescribed operating and safety standards that are followed at general-aviation airports. A DC-3 (left) and an L-18 Lodestar occupy the Atlantic Aviation Corporation ramp. (H. V. Reilly/NJAHOF.)

HONORING THE PIONEERS. Wearing some of their original flight gear, Teterboro Airport pioneers William Diehl (back, left) and Clarence D. Chamberlin climb aboard a 1920s model of a French fleet biplane while a group of officials pose in front of them. Standing from left to right are Henry Esposito of Atlantic Aviation Corporation; Bergen County Sheriff Joe Job; Francis Gerard, director of aeronautics for the State of New Jersey; O. J. Studeman, vice president of Pan Am; and H. V. "Pat" Riley, public relations for Pan Am. (H. V. Reilly/NJAHOF.)

RETIRING PAN AM VICE PRESIDENT. Studeman (foreground) and his staff from the Pan Am Metropolitan Air Facilities Division are pictured at his retirement in 1972. On the far right is H. V. "Pat" Reilly, the future executive director of the Aviation Hall of Fame and Museum at Teterboro. At the time of this photograph, he was Pan Am's public relations director. (H. V. Reilly/NJAHOF.)

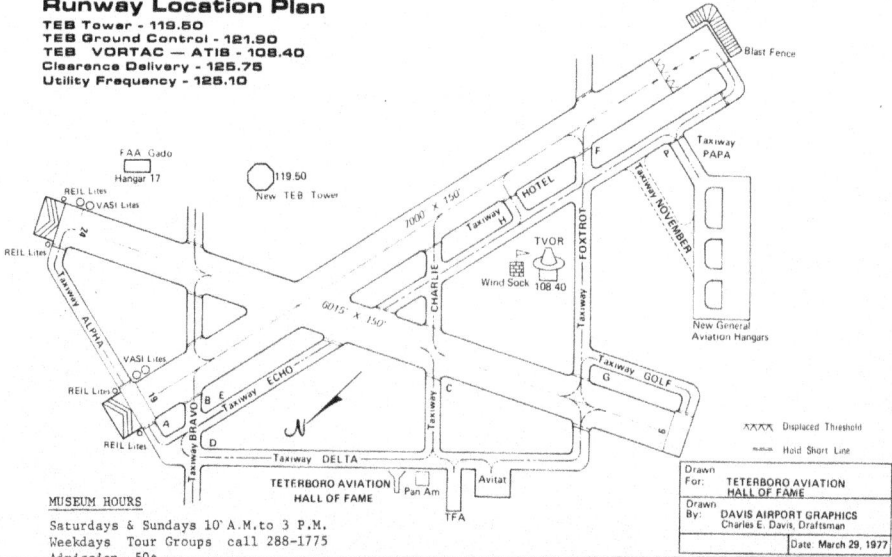

TETERBORO AVIATION HALL OF FAME

Teterboro Airport
Runway Location Plan

TEB Tower - 119.50
TEB Ground Control - 121.90
TEB VORTAC — ATIS - 108.40
Clearance Delivery - 125.75
Utility Frequency - 125.10

Drawn For:	TETERBORO AVIATION HALL OF FAME
Drawn By:	DAVIS AIRPORT GRAPHICS Charles E. Davis, Draftsman
	Date: March 29, 1977

MUSEUM HOURS

Saturdays & Sundays 10 A.M.to 3 P.M.
Weekdays Tour Groups call 288-1775
Admission 50¢

AIRPORT LAYOUT. This March 1977 airport layout shows no development on the east side of the field other than the new tower. In the decades that followed, Dassault-Falcon, Signature Flight Support, and other FBOs established themselves on the east side of the field. The expanded Aviation Hall of Fame and Museum at Teterboro would also relocate there. (NJAHOF.)

AVIATION HALL OF FAME AND MUSEUM. This was Teterboro's first permanent control tower. It opened in 1948. When it was retired, it became the first home of the Aviation Hall of Fame and Museum at Teterboro and incorporated as a nonprofit educational organization on April 6, 1972. There were 100 steps from the field level up to the top of the tower. The hall of fame occupied the top three floors. (NJAHOF.)

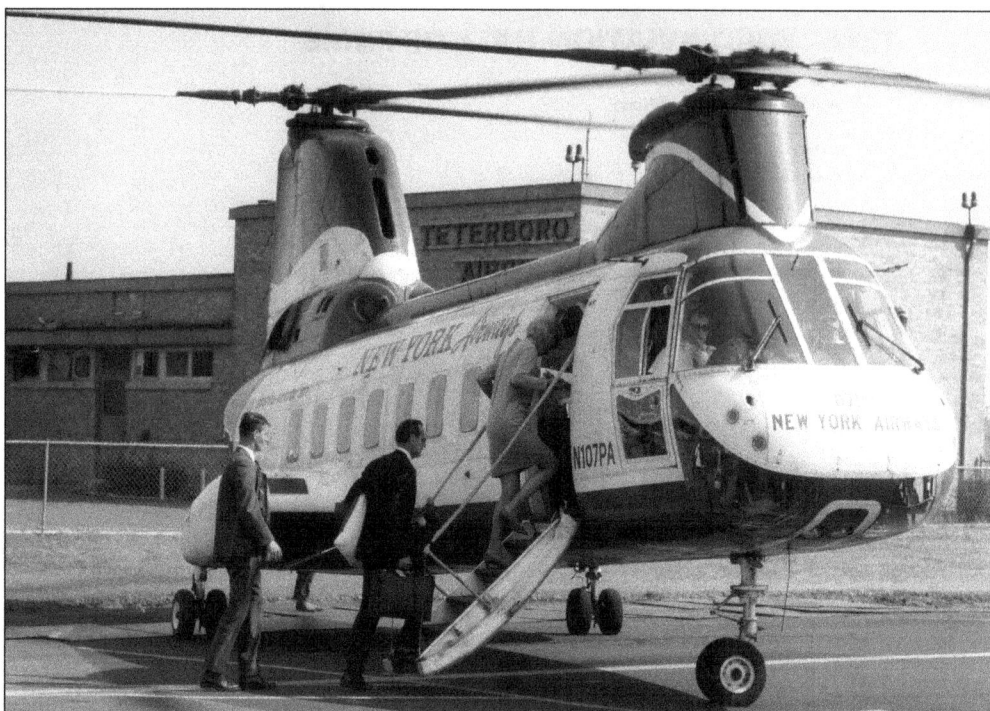

NEW YORK AIRWAYS. In October 1967, New York Airways, the first scheduled helicopter service in the United States, inaugurated 20 daily, scheduled helicopter flights from Teterboro Airport to LaGuardia, John F. Kennedy International, Newark, and Morristown Airports. A second attempt was made on January 8, 1974. Scheduled airline service never caught on because Newark Airport was larger and had a well-developed infrastructure. The Boeing Vertol 107 could carry 25 passengers. (NJAHOF.)

NEW FACILITIES. According to records, this is an artist's rendition of a possible new terminal area at Teterboro Airport. It was to provide convenient check-in facilities for passengers and baggage, helicopter shuttle service to the John F. Kennedy International Airport terminal, and serve corporate aircraft. Pan Am operated Teterboro Airport for the port authority. (NJAHOF.)

VOLKSWAGEN CORPORATE JET. Two twin-engine Saberliners are parked on the Atlantic Aviation Corporation ramp in this 1970s photograph. D-CEVW (foreground) belonged to the Volkswagen Company and was based at Teterboro Airport. The turboprop in the upper left is turning off taxiway Charlie and onto the Atlantic Aviation ramp. (NJAHOF.)

CORPORATE JETS AT ATLANTIC AVIATION. In the 1970s, corporate jets began to crowd out the older turboprops. In the foreground, from front to back, is a Gulfstream 1 (G-1). Alongside it is N907R, a Rockwell International Corporation NA-265-65; followed by N48UC, a deHavilland DH125; N810PA, a Dassault-Breguet Falcon 20EW; and N1234X, a Cessna 501 Citation 1 SP. (NJAHOF.)

GATHERING OF EAGLES. Pictured from left to right are Fred Wehran, Dean Smith, Herbert O. Fisher, Charles Wittemann, William Diehl, and Clarence D. Chamberlin. Wehran, a World War I Marine Corps pilot, was a former owner of the airport. Smith started his career at Hadley Field in 1925 as an airmail pilot. Fisher was a test pilot and flew for 60 years. Wittemann built the first airplane factory, and Diehl was the first pilot to land on the field. (H. V. Reilly/NJAHOF.)

ARTIST'S RENDITION. This is the future aviation hall of fame, as envisioned by artist's rendition. The painting was presented on July 3, 1979, when Gov. Brendan Byrne signed the bill establishing the Aviation Hall of Fame and Museum of New Jersey. Byrne, in an encore, returned to the annual dinner in 2009. (NJAHOF.)

LINDBERGH AVIATION CENTER. On September 10, 1980, the Lindbergh Aviation Center opened at the south end of the airport off Moonachie Avenue. It included two hangars and a passenger terminal constructed by the Falcon Jet Corporation and a hangar/office complex leased by Aero Services. Pan Am invested an additional $1.9 million for the construction of two taxiways and approximately six acres of aircraft ramps. (NJAHOF.)

OPENING DAY. Pictured at the opening of the Lindbergh Aviation Center at Teterboro Airport from left to right are Orlando "Dit" Panfile, president, Aero services; Alan Sager, chairman of the port authority; and John Kennedy, vice president, Pan Am. The plaque and center are an acknowledgement of Charles A. and Anne Morrow Lindbergh's daring and historic achievements, some of which took place at Teterboro. (H. V. Riley/NJAHOF.)

OLD TOWER AND MUSEUM. The first museum reached capacity when it held about 1,000 artifacts. "People gave me things all the time, but I had no place left for them," H. V. "Pat" Reilly, the director emeritus said. "I've ran out of every corner." Among the artifacts in the first museum were early aircraft instruments, a 1918 mahogany propeller used on a Liberty engine manufactured by Curtiss-Wright Corporation, and sheepskin-lined flying boots worn by aviation pioneer Bert Acosta in 1927. (Author's collection.)

SPIRIT OF AMERICA. In 1982, National Distillers's Teterboro-based Gulfstream III *Spirit of America* established a world record for corporate jets when it flew around the world in 47 hours, 39 minutes. The flight established a new record time for corporate aircraft. The Teterboro-based jet shaved more than 10 hours off the old mark of 57 hours, 26 minutes set by professional golfer Arnold Palmer in a Lear 36 in 1976. (Author's collection.)

SPIRIT OF AMERICA CREW. Harold Curtis, manager of the company's air transport division, chief pilot William Mack, and assistant chief pilot Robert Dannhardt piloted the airplane, the first production model of the Gulfstream III. Here Curtis (left) and Mack are performing a checklist prior to their departure from Teterboro Airport. The aircraft made six fuel stops on its 23,490-mile circumnavigation of the earth before returning to Teterboro. (NJAHOF.)

NEW JERSEY AVIATION CENTER. When the new aviation hall of fame and museum opened in 1983, it was soon overwhelmed with artifacts, and plans were made for an expansion. Building the extension was delayed several years, as studies were made to determine if the expansion would damage the nearby wetlands. (Author's collection.)

STATIC AIR SHOW. For years, Teterboro Airport was a magnet for air shows. As air traffic increased and homes began to crowd the airport, the shows were cut back to static displays of war birds, general aviation, and aerobatic airplanes. In this aerial photograph taken around 1984, the B-17 Flying Fortress *Texas Raiders* is on display. (NJAHOF.)

NOISE ABATEMENT. From left to right, Teterboro Airport manager Phil Engle, assembly representative Ben Mazur, and Nick Felice discuss the newly installed noise-monitoring system. As the community around Teterboro began to grow and as jet aircraft came on the scene, noise became a major issue for the airport's management. Teterboro became the first to install a noise monitoring system at a general-aviation airport. Eventually flight restrictions and curfews reduced some of the noise. (H. V. Reilly/NJAHOF.)

JUNE 20, 1987. On June 20, 1987, three Frenchmen and a Canadian took off from Teterboro Airport on the last leg of their recreation of Howard Hughes's 1938 flight around the world. This Lockheed 18-Lodestar, a contemporary of Hughes's airplane, arrived in Paris the following morning. It broke Hughes's record of 91 hours, 17 minutes, completing the journey in 88 hours, 44 minutes. (H. V. Reilly/NJAHOF.)

LOCKHEED 18-LODESTAR. The 42-foot-long Lockheed 18-Lodestar had a 60-foot wingspan and, as modified, matched Howard Hughes's original aircraft down to the 36,000 ping-pong balls to keep the airplane afloat in case it crashed into the ocean. The pilot, Patrick Fourticq, spent two years looking for an airplane similar to Hughes's aircraft, and the crew spent 5,000 hours refitting it. (H. V. Reilly/NJAHOF.)

DEDICATION OF THE FRED WEHRAN PAVILION, C. 1988. Fred Wehran (light jacket) flew Scout seaplanes for the Marine Corps during World War I. In 1941, Wehran made a $10,000 down payment on the $50,000, 500-acre marshy tract known as Teterboro Airport. At the time, the tract surrounded a seldom-used sod runway. In 1949, Wehran sold the airport to the port authority for $3.2 million. (H. V. Reilly/NJAHOF.)

MODERN-DAY TETERBORO AIRPORT. Teterboro is the nearest general-aviation airport to Midtown Manhattan. Its preferential runway 1-19 is instrument landing system equipped and is 7,000 feet long; runway 6-24 is 6,015 feet long. Pan Am's initial plans for development of Teterboro Airport called for an ultra-modern facility to meet the needs of general aviation and constructed at the south end of the field. (H. V. Reilly/NJAHOF.)

GULFSTREAM I TAKING OFF. Today Teterboro handles no commercial or scheduled air traffic. It is a general-aviation "reliever" airport, which takes pressure off other area airports. On December 1, 2000, the port authority assumed day-to-day operations. For noise abatement, its two runways are restricted to aircraft weighing no more than 100,000 pounds, and there is a nighttime curfew. (NJAHOF.)

GATHERING OF AUTHORS. From left to right are William (Bill) Rhode, H. V. "Pat" Reilly, and the author around 1993. Rhode, inducted into the hall of fame in 1984, was a daredevil aviator, parachutist, and aviation historian, who in 1940 set a record of jumping with five parachutes. The record stood until 1990. Reilly cofounded the Aviation Hall of Fame and Museum at Teterboro in 1972. Reilly was inducted into the hall of fame in 1993 and today is the director emeritus. (Author's collection.)

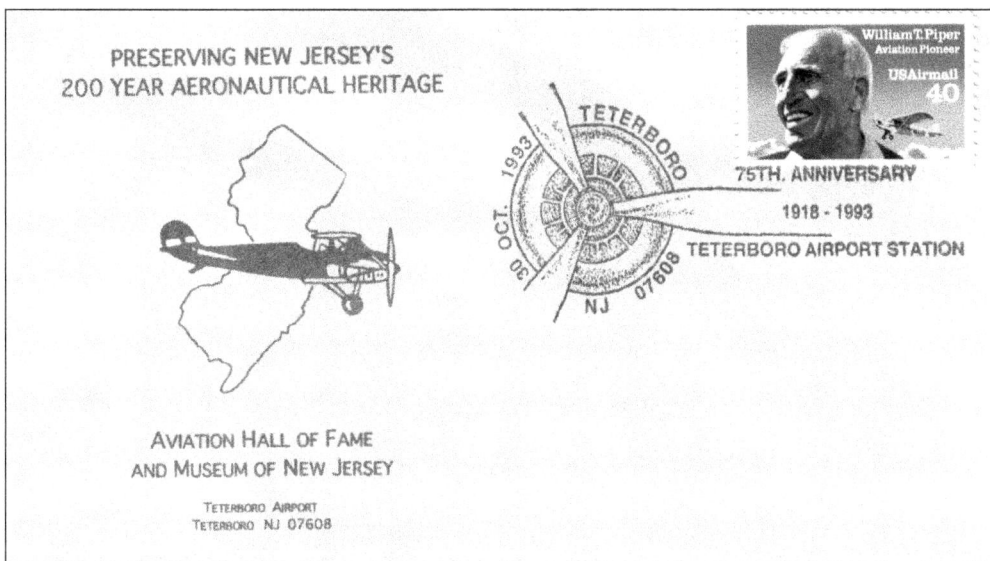

TETERBORO AIRPORT 75TH ANNIVERSARY. On October 30–31, 1993, Teterboro Airport celebrated its 75th anniversary with this envelope. For the two-day celebration, the organizers created a historical perspective with vintage World War II warbirds and a photographic exhibit tracing 200 years of aviation history in New Jersey. As the oldest continually active airport in the state, it played a significant role in development and advancement of that history. (Author's collection.)

HADLEY FIELD MARKER. Although Hadley Field lost out to Newark Airport to fly the mail, the 77-acre airport remained open until 1968, catering to mostly private aircraft. Today all that remains of it is this marker. Teterboro survived to serve corporate aircraft because it was closer to New York City, which made it convenient for access to Manhattan. (NJAHOF.)

SNOW STORM, C. 1996. The worst blizzard in decades shut down the big three airports—Newark, John F. Kennedy International, and La Guardia. No air traffic moved along the Northeastern seaboard, except at Teterboro Airport. To keep runway 6-24 open and a taxiway cleared, more than a dozen people worked around the clock, operating a 28-foot plow and two snow-blowing machines, which continually scraped the main runway. (NJAHOF.)

MUSEUM EXPANSION. Tucked away on the east side of Teterboro Airport is the $625,000 expansion, a 6,000-square foot, two-story building. The new educational center, dedicated on September 27, 1997, created room for some 10,000 artifacts. Approximately 5,000 visitors come to the museum every year, with an additional 6,000 visitors to the annual Wings and Wheels Expo held each fall. (Author's collection.)

HURRICANE FLOYD, THE DAY AFTER. Hurricane Floyd crossed New Jersey and hit Teterboro Airport on September 17, 1999. Floyd left almost 14 inches of water on the airport and in the surrounding community. Power was out in some areas for more than a week, and dozens of aircraft suffered serious damage from the floodwaters. (Allisandra Joy Fairclough/NJAHOF.)

NOISE TESTS. In 1968, six towns in the immediate area of the airport sued for noise complaints. Here a turbine-powered aircraft is taxiing past the new hangars off Moonachie Avenue. A truck is measuring the decibel output of the turbine engines. Eventually, with increasing jet traffic, there were community rallies and legislation to curb the airport's operating hours and weight limits on airplanes. (NJAHOF.)

New Hangars. Four new general-aviation hangars at the south end of Teterboro Airport off Moonachie Avenue are seen almost complete and will soon be open for tenants. Each hangar is 200 feet long and 95 feet wide. Ceiling clearance is 30 feet, and the hangar doors open to 130 feet. The office space is air-conditioned, and the service area for aircraft maintenance is mechanically ventilated. (NJAHOF.)

Student Pilot. While Teterboro Airport has been the scene of countless sightseeing and pilot-training flights, its proximity to the large, commercial airports has forced these operations to smaller airports. Student pilots, with an hour to fly, could not afford to spend 30 minutes on the ramp waiting for traffic to clear so they could take off. They eventually migrated to other airports such as Essex County and Morristown, where they could take off immediately. (H. V. Reilly/NJAHOF.)

H. V. "Pat" Reilly. At a party on August 14, 1970, commemorating the 50th anniversary of the first landing at Teterboro Airport, H. V. "Pat" Reilly (pictured), Donald Borg, publisher of New Jersey's largest evening newspaper, the *Record*, and others nostalgically discussed the events that had taken place at the airport. It was soon obvious that the airport held a unique historical significance. The group agreed to preserve the history, and the seed of the hall of fame and museum began to grow. (Author's collection.)

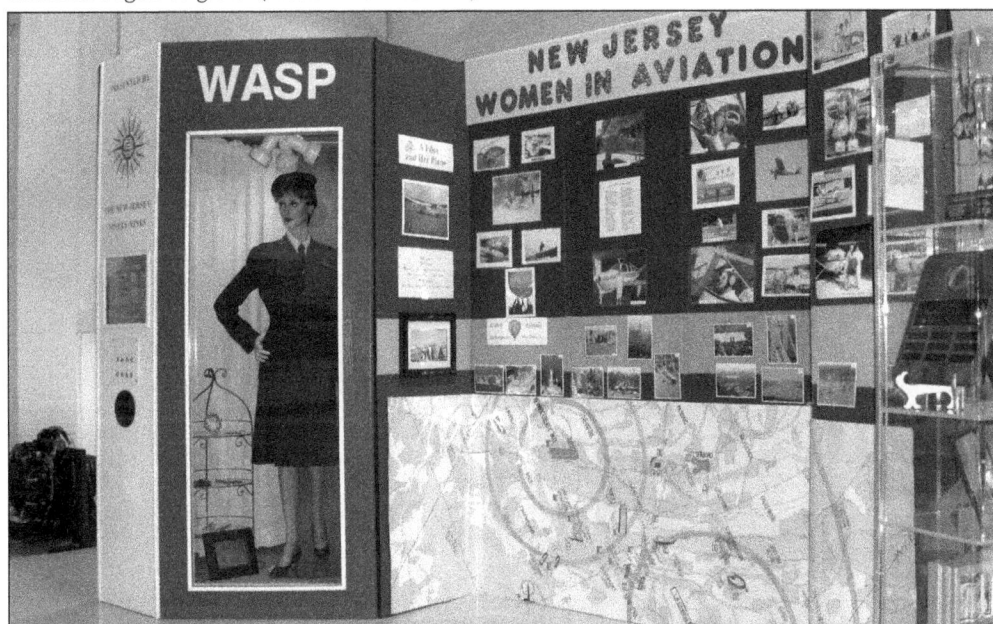

Museum Interior. In today's museum, there is an exhibit featuring New Jersey women in aviation. The space section includes a space suit worn by one of the original seven Mercury astronauts, Walter Schirra; a glove worn by New Jersey astronaut Buzz Aldrin Jr.; a wheel from a moon rover; artifacts from the Hindenburg dirigible accident in 1937; and more. (Author's collection.)

WRIGHT ENGINES. Wright Aeronautical Corporation manufactured engines that powered U.S. bombers and fighter aircraft in World War II. Some of the engines such as the Wright L-5 Whirlwind (right), which powered many of Fokker's airplanes; the Wright Tornado R-2160; and the Wright R-1820 Cyclone (left) are on display at the aviation hall of fame, including photographs from the factories where they were made. (Author's collection.)

HALL OF FAME ROOM. The New Jersey Aviation Hall of Fame and Museum, founded in 1972, was the first state aviation hall of fame in the nation. Its goal is to preserve the state's 216 years of aviation and space history. There are currently 158 New Jersey aviation greats inducted in the hall of fame, including 22 New Jersey war aces and six New Jersey–born astronauts. (Author's collection.)

124

EARLY TETERBORO PHOTOGRAPH. This photograph, taken in the 1970s, shows runway 1-19 intersecting 6-24. The Atlantic Aviation Corporation hangar No. 3 is off to the right with the first permanent control tower visible on its right. Because of several accidents, runway 6-24 now has a 250-foot arrestor bed at the end of the runway. (NJAHOF.)

FRED FELDMAN. Fred Feldman was the second helicopter pilot in the United States to provide radio traffic reports. Francis Gary Powers, the U-2 pilot shot down over the Soviet Union in 1960, was the first for a Los Angeles station. Flying for New York radio station WOR but based in Teterboro, Feldman spent 16 years monitoring traffic for rush-hour commuters. He invented the term "rubbernecking delays" to explain why commuters would be late for work or dinner. (NJAHOF.)

ARON "DUKE" KRANTZ. When Aron "Duke" Krantz was chief test pilot for Bendix Aviation Corporation, he put the DC-3 Flying Showcase on a cross-country tour, flying to aviation events to display and discuss Bendix products. The Bendix aircraft were first located in the old Wright aeronautical hangar located near the Bendix plant but later moved across Industrial Avenue to the Atlantic Aviation Corporation hangar. (NJAHOF.)

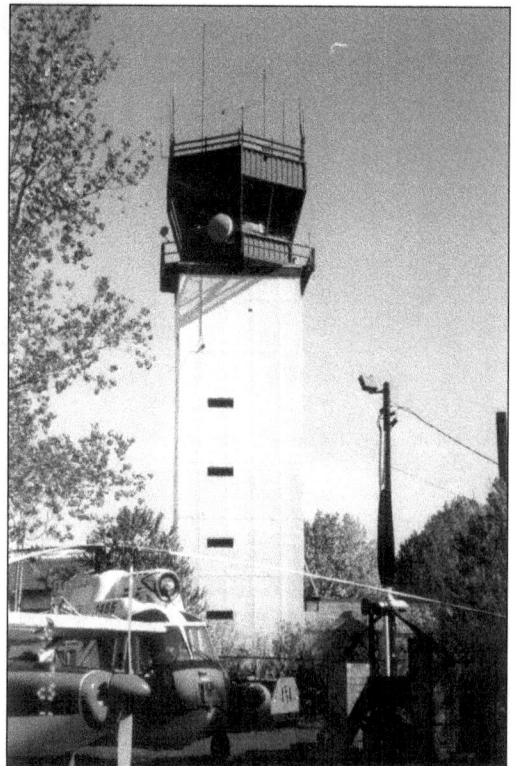

NEW CONTROL TOWER. The newest control tower, built on the east side of the airport by the FAA, went into operation on October 29, 1975. Immediately to its left is the aviation hall of fame and museum. The U.S. Coast Guard donated the Sikorsky HH-52A helicopter to the museum. (NJAHOF.)

PAN AM CREW. When Pan Am took over the management of the field in 1970, the change was also reflected in its personnel. Pilots and flight attendants were professional in appearance, conduct, and competence. Pan Am was the North American marketing agent for Dassault-Falcon Jet. N813PA was a Dassault-Falcon 20 and is seen here at John F. Kennedy International Airport. (NJAHOF.)

NEWARK AIRPORT. As migration from New York City and light industry began to encroach on Teterboro Airport, its opportunities to expand became severely limited. Newark Airport, on the other hand, was also built on meadowlands but grew almost since its first days in 1928. Today it occupies 2,027 acres. This photograph of Newark Airport shows the 580-room Marriot Hotel. Behind it is terminal C, which did not open with the satellite terminals. (NJAHOF.)

Visit us at
arcadiapublishing.com

······································